Creative
MACHINE
STITCHING

Special Effects for Quilts and More

PATRICIA NELSON

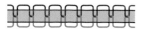

Balanced Tension

Fig. 1

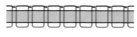

Top Tension Too Tight

Fig. 2

Top Tension Too Loose

Fig. 3

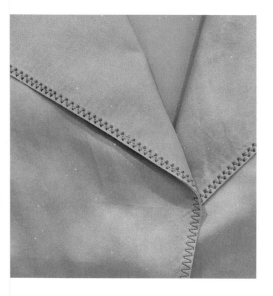

A basic utility stitch with tension manipulation creates an elegant, decorative trim!

scrap fabric in half to create a double layer; stitch across it. If your tension is balanced, the upper and lower threads will lock between the fabric layers (fig. 1).

If you can see little dots of bobbin thread between the stitches on the right side of the fabric, the top tension is too tight (fig. 2). Loosen the tension control by half a number and test again. If necessary, continue to adjust the tension half a number at a time until the bobbin thread no longer shows.

Turn your test sample over and look at the reverse side of your row of stitches. If you can see little dots of the top thread showing through, the top tension is too loose (fig. 3). Tighten the top tension in half-number increments until a balanced tension is achieved.

If adjusting the tension dial does not correct the problem, check to be sure the same weight thread is in the bobbin and on top. Also, check the needle size; a needle that's too large for the fabric and thread can create an unbalanced stitch. For example, using a size 100/16 needle with quilting cotton will leave a hole large enough to alter the stitch balance. A size 75/11 is more appropriate.

This discussion reveals that if you want the bobbin thread to show on the right side of the fabric for decorative purposes, you should tighten the top tension until the desired effect is achieved. You can see the results on the collar of the blouse shown at left. The border was stitched with a multiple stitch zigzag using rayon threads. The top thread color matches the blouse fabric and the bobbin thread color creates contrast. A tight top tension brings the contrasting color to the surface to create the unique texture.

SETTING UP

EACH TECHNIQUE presented in this book requires a different combination of threads, needles, and tension settings to achieve the desired effect. I provide guidelines for each technique and instructions to help you work through a sample piece before starting a project. Practice the following suggestions as you perfect each technique.

⟡ Make sure the presser foot and the thread take-up lever are in the up position when threading or you will get a big tangled mess on the bottom of your work when you start to sew.

⟡ Always bring the bobbin thread up to the top of your work and hold both threads before starting to sew. On some of the newer machines it isn't necessary to bring the thread up, but do hold the top thread when starting to sew. Consult your machine manual or your machine dealer if you're in doubt about how to bring the thread to the top.

- For those of us with mature eyesight, here's a hint for threading the needle that I learned from Georgia Bonesteel. Cut the thread at an angle, hold the thread between your forefingers, and aim for the needle's eye. You can also try holding a piece of white paper behind the needle to help illuminate the eye.

- During the stitching process, if you need to rotate the work, stop with the needle down in the fabric. If your machine has a needle-up, needle-down function, use it. This will keep your work from sliding away.

Hold the thread between your forefingers and aim for the needle's eye.

Staying Comfortable While You Sew

SITTING IN the correct position at the sewing machine will enable you to sew longer and be more comfortable at the same time. Your body should be positioned in front of the sewing machine so that the needle is exactly at the center of your chest. Adjust your chair so that your arms are bent at the elbow at a 90° angle, your wrists are in a straight line, and your shoulders are in a relaxed position when you are guiding a piece of fabric through the machine. The palms of your hands should lie flat on the sewing machine bed.

I have taught myself to sew with my left foot mainly because I need to use my right leg to maneuver the knee lever on my Bernina, but I have noticed a benefit. By alternating the foot I sew with, I've found I am able to sew for longer periods of time because I am constantly distributing my weight between both hip areas. Using both feet at the same time is even more comfortable.

You can use several stretching exercises to relieve muscle tension caused by long sessions at the sewing machine. For one, place your right arm across your chest, with your right hand on your left shoulder. With your left hand behind the right elbow, push your arm around your neck for a gentle stretch. Hold your arm in this position for 20 seconds; repeat for the left arm. Do this several times.

Another exercise consists of standing up, bending over at the waist, and just hanging for several moments.

Like driving, sewing is best if you take a break every two hours. Go have a cup of tea, run an errand, or take a short walk. When you return, your frame of mind will be better than ever and your eyes will be focused!

Embroidery Supplies

THIS SECTION COVERS the basic materials and tools necessary for the embroidery techniques presented in this book, as well as how to use them to produce the best results during the embroidery process. Instructions with each project will identify the specific materials needed to make that item. If you have trouble finding these materials locally, refer to "Resources" on page 111 for mail-order companies.

THREADS

I CONFESS, I love thread and am embarrassed to say how much I have—but I really do use it all! Threads suitable for machine embroidery come in all kinds of fibers, weights, and colors. Even all-purpose sewing thread can be used. Don't limit your thread shopping to the fabric store, either; lots of wonderful threads and yarns are available at craft, yarn, and needlework shops.

Thread sizing is not universal among thread types or between threads manufactured for the home sewer and those manufactured for industrial purposes. This may seem confusing at first, but since you control the density of the stitched design by how many rows of stitching you lay down on the fabric, thread size is only an issue when you're determining the correct needle size, stabilizer, and tension. We'll cover needles and stabilizers later in this section; for tension adjustments, refer to "Understanding Tension" on page 5. If you're interested in learning more about how threads are made and sized, YLI Corporation offers a brochure, "A Thread of Truth," that can be downloaded from the company's Web site at www.ylicorp.com. This 32-page booklet contains factual information about sewing thread, as well as machine needles, and includes a chart for selecting the proper needle for each thread type. If you don't have Internet access, the brochure is available by calling 800-296-8139.

The following is a list of some of the more popular threads used for embroidery:

- **Rayon** threads are beautiful and silky with a high luster. They are delicate and not as durable as polyester or cotton embroidery threads. Rayon threads come in three weights; the lower the number, the thicker the thread. The 40-weight thread is the thread used most often for embroidery; 35-weight rayon thread is often called rayon twist because it is actually two different colors of thread twisted together; and 30-weight thread is one-third thicker than 40 weight. Use a 75/11 or 90/14 embroidery needle, depending on your fabric and thread thickness.

- **Polyester** thread comes in 40 weight for embroidery and 60 weight for the bobbin and is available in a variety of colors. It is comparable to rayon in luster, but it is stronger, more durable, more colorfast, and it is bleach resistant. Use a 75/11 embroidery needle.

- **Cotton** embroidery threads are strong and durable. The higher the number, the finer the thread. If you want to fill a design quickly, choose a 30- or 40-weight thread. A 50-weight thread is good for garment construction as well as embroidery, while a finer 60-weight thread is a good choice for delicate fabrics and the bobbin if a project is reversible and a color match is needed. For 50- and 60-weight threads, choose a 75/11 or an 80/12 universal needle; use an 80/12 or larger topstitching needle for 30- and 40-weight threads.

- **Cotton-and-polyester** threads are made by wrapping a cotton thread around a polyester core thread. They come in 50 and 60 weights, as well as a thicker topstitching weight. The 50-weight thread is normally used for all-purpose sewing but can be used for embroidery. The 60-weight thread can be used for embroidery or as a lightweight bobbin thread when a color match is needed on the reverse side of a project. Use a 75/11 or an 80/12 universal needle for the 50- and 60-weight threads; the topstitching thread requires a large-eye needle such as the 90/14 topstitching needle to prevent shredding.

- **Metallic** threads are delicate and beautiful to work with. They are available in a selection of sizes and textures. Use a 90/14 metallic needle or an 80/12 topstitching needle, and place the spools in an upright position when stitching. If breakage is a problem, loosen the top thread tension. If you loosen the tension so that the thread does not break but the tension is not balanced (that is, the top thread shows on the reverse side), try using a lighter-weight bobbin thread. If the thread breaks after loosening the top tension and using bobbin thread, place a cotton swab in front of the first thread guide from the thread spool and tape it in place. Moisten the cotton tip with a silicone lubricant; then place a second lubricated cotton swab on top of the

TIP

For reversible projects, use the same thread in the bobbin as on top.

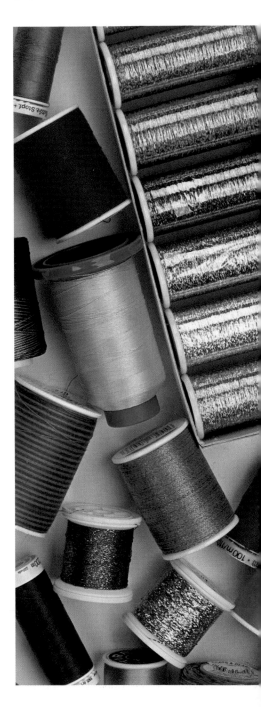

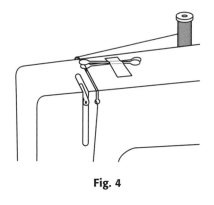

Fig. 4

first swab and tape it in place. Now thread the machine, guiding the thread between the tips of the two swabs (fig. 4). This works like magic for me! A silicone lubricant may harm some machines, though, so be sure to check with your sewing machine dealer before using one.

✧ **Silk** threads are strong and very durable, and they reflect the light. Dry cleaning is recommended for projects with silk thread as they may bleed when washed. Use an 80/12 universal needle or a 70/11 Sharp needle.

All the threads in the preceding list can be used in the top, but you'll notice that the threads available in finer weights can also be used in the bobbin. For most of the techniques in this book, you will need to use a finer thread in the bobbin than in the needle to prevent a buildup of thread on the wrong side of the fabric. In addition to those mentioned here, there are threads marketed specifically for the bobbin, which now come in many colors. Bobbin thread is also available on prewound bobbins. Check with your dealer before using them to see if they are compatible with your machine.

Spool Positions

NOT ALL THREADS are wound on the spool the same way. Some are cross-wound while others are straight wound, or stacked (fig. 5). The manner in which the threads are wound onto the spool will affect the way they unwind and pass through the tension disks and needle. Proper positioning will help eliminate any added twists in the thread and keep your embroidery smooth.

The general rule is that cross-wound thread spools should be placed on a horizontal spool holder; straight-wound or stacked thread spools should be placed in an upright position. Some sewing machines come with both types of spool holders; if yours does not, adapters are available from most sewing notions mail-order catalogs. Consider using a thread stand for cross-wound spools that are too large for the spool holder and for slippery straight-wound threads that pool at the bottom of the spool and twist around the spool pin.

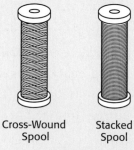

Cross-Wound Spool   Stacked Spool

Fig. 5

NEEDLES

LIKE THREAD, needles now come in a plethora of types to meet the creative demands of every sewer. Whether for quilting, embroidering, or using metallic thread, a specific needle is available to produce ideal results.

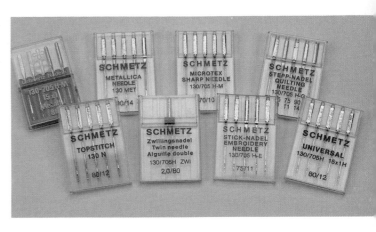

Needle Types

The following list describes the needles you will use most often for the techniques and projects in this book. Each of these needles comes in several sizes. To select the correct size for your project, you will need to consider the fabric you will be stitching on and the thread you will be using. Using the proper needle will reduce thread breakage and skipped stitches, thus making your sewing much more enjoyable. The size of each needle type is marked on the needle shank as well as the needle case. You will notice two numbers: the first is the European size, the second is the American size. The general rule is this: the finer the fabric, the finer the needle. Refer to figure 6 for a visual aid that shows the parts of a sewing machine needle.

There's a needle for every job!

◈ **Embroidery** needles have a larger eye and a specially designed scarf to prevent shredding and breakage when sewing dense embroidery designs with rayon, metallic, and other machine embroidery threads. They are available in sizes 75/11 and 90/14 and also as a twin needle.

◈ **Metallic** needles have an elongated, coated eye; a deeper front groove; and a sharp point to prevent metallic threads from shredding. You can find them under the names Metallica (Schmetz), Metafil (Lammertz), and Metallic Machine Embroidery (Madeira). They are available in sizes 70/10 through 90/14 and also as a twin needle.

◈ **Quilting** needles have a tapered point to successfully sew through multiple layers and crossed seams without damaging the fabrics. You can find these needles in sizes 75/11 and 90/14.

◈ **Sharp** needles are a good choice for tightly woven fabrics, lightweight fabrics, and delicate wovens. The shaft on these needles is thin and the point is sharp to pierce the fabrics without damage. They are available in sizes ranging from 60/8 to 100/16.

◈ **Topstitch** needles should be used when working with multiple threads, topstitching thread, or thicker threads. They have an extra-large eye and a larger groove to accommodate the additional thickness, and the point is extra sharp for piercing the fabric without leaving a large hole. You can find them in sizes 70/10 to 100/16.

◈ **Universal** needles are all-purpose needles. The needle point is slightly rounded to accommodate knit fabrics, and yet sharp enough to pierce woven fabrics. Look for them in sizes 60/8 through 120/19.

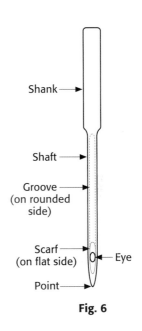

Shank →

Shaft →

Groove (on rounded side)

Scarf (on flat side) → ← Eye

Point →

Fig. 6

TIPS

❖

*Remember the thread rule:
the eye of the needle should
be twice the size of the
thread(s) going through it.*

❖

*Whenever I hear a popping
sound as the needle enters
the fabric, I know it's time
for a new needle.*

Sewing with Twin Needles

Twin needles are great for creating special effects with built-in stitches and free-motion stitching. The sizing is slightly different, however, than with a single needle. Two numbers are listed on the needle case; the first number is the distance between the needles and the second number is the European needle size. For example, a twin-needle size 2.5/80 means the needles are 2.5 millimeters apart and they are size 80 European (12 American).

When using and threading twin needles, always check with your machine dealer for the recommended threading procedure. If none is available, determine whether the thread spools must be on side-by-side spindles. If they must, place the spools so that they unwind in opposite directions to prevent them from rubbing against each other. Also, place the threads on either side of the tension disk, if possible, and thread the right-hand thread in the right needle and the left-hand thread in the left needle (fig. 7). If the threads twist and break while sewing, thread only one of them through the last thread guide, leaving the other one outside the guide. Loosen the tension to achieve flat stitches.

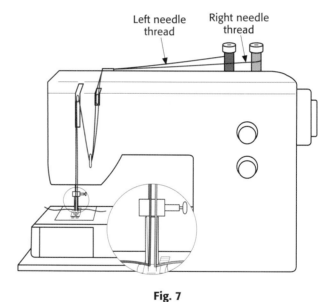

Left needle thread   Right needle thread

Fig. 7

If your machine has a twin-needle function button, engage it whenever you plan on using multiple needles with any stitch other than a straight stitch. This helps prevent the needles from swinging wider than the width possible for your machine foot, avoiding needle breakage and possible damage to your machine and fabrics.

Presser Feet

MOST OF the feet necessary for the projects in this book probably came with your machine; if not, check with your machine dealer regarding availability. You will need a darning foot for free-motion stitching, an appliqué foot (open-toe is preferable) and a zigzag foot for built-in stitch embroidery, a ¼" foot for sewing accurate seams, and a walking foot for stitching through multiple layers of fabric. We will explore specialty feet such as the gimping foot, fringe foot, and candlewicking foot in "Special Effects" beginning on page 89.

The correct foot makes creative stitching a breeze!

Hoops

HOOPS ARE essential tools for beautiful embroidery. They hold the fabric taut and help prevent puckering. Two types of hoops are available, either a spring hoop or a screw-type hoop. The spring hoop consists of two pieces: a plastic ring and a C-shaped metal ring with handles that fits inside the plastic ring. I use either a 5"- or 7"-diameter spring hoop for all my projects that can be hooped because I can unhoop my project easily, move the hoop to another area, and rehoop without removing the entire project from under the needle. Screw-type hoops are available in wood or plastic. They consist of two rings, one solid and one that can be opened and closed with a screw attachment. I prefer a thin wooden hoop with a slotted screw because it is easier to slide under the needle, and the slotted screw is easy to tighten with a tiny screwdriver.

Some fabrics should not be hooped, either because they are too thick, too stretchy, or too delicate. For these fabrics, I use the hoopless method, which involves using a screw hoop in conjunction with an adhesive stabilizer (refer to "The Hoopless Method" on page 15).

TIP

Use the smallest hoop you can for your project, to help prevent distortion and puckering.

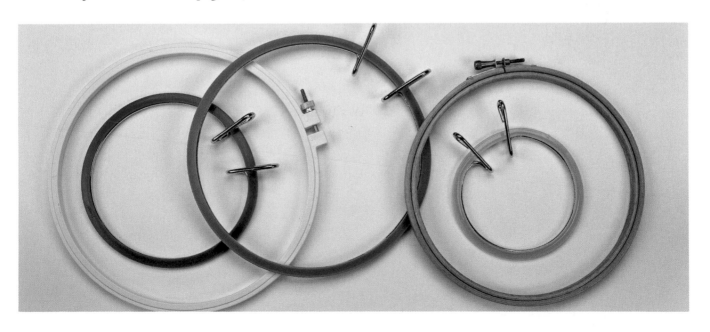

Hooping Your Fabric

The hooping process is relatively the same for both spring hoops and screw-type hoops. To use a spring hoop, place the plastic ring on a flat surface and place the fabric to be embroidered right side up over it, centering the design area inside the ring. Next, take the C-shaped ring, squeeze the handles together, and place it over the fabric and into the plastic ring.

Plastic Ring

Fabric over Ring

C-Shaped Ring Inserted
into Plastic Ring

The fabric should fit snugly into the hoop and be taut, like a drum. If the fabric is not taut, it means the C-shaped ring is loose. To tighten the ring, stretch it open by grabbing the handles and spreading them apart. Be careful not to tighten the ring and stretch the fabric too much because it may distort the embroidery.

Spread apart handles to increase
tension in plastic hoop.

To hoop your fabric in a screw-type hoop, loosen the screw on the ring with the screw attachment and place the ring on a flat surface. Center the area of the item to be embroidered right side up over the ring. Place the closed ring over the fabric and push it into the bottom ring, loosening the screw more if necessary. When the fabric is taut in the hoop, tighten the screw to secure the fabric. Be careful not to stretch the fabric too much or the embroidery may become distorted.

Ring with
Screw Attachment

Fabric over Ring

Closed Ring Inserted
into Screw Ring

TIP

❖

Do not leave fabric hooped when you are not working on the project, because a permanent ring mark, also known as hoop burn, could be left in the fabric. It's a good idea to pretest your fabric to make sure hoop marks created during the embroidery process will disappear after washing or ironing.

The Hoopless Method

For stretchy and delicate fabrics, or fabric that can't or shouldn't be hooped, you'll want to use this method. Although it is called "hoopless," you still need a screw-type hoop, as well as an adhesive-backed stabilizer; the fabric isn't inserted into the hoop, but the hoop is used as a vehicle for holding the stabilizer on which the fabric is placed.

There are two methods for using a hoop with adhesive stabilizer. For both methods, cut a square of adhesive-backed stabilizer that is slightly larger than the hoop.

For the first method, place the two rings of the hoop together and tighten the screw so they do not separate. Remove the backing from the stabilizer and place the entire hoop directly onto the adhesive side. Smooth the area of the fabric to be embroidered onto the adhesive, centering it as necessary.

Sticky Stabilizer under
Screw-Type Hoop

Smooth fabric onto adhesive.

For the second method, hoop the stabilizer with the paper backing side up. Using a seam ripper, pin, or other sharp object, score the paper backing and peel it away from inside the hoop. Place the fabric to be embroidered onto the adhesive, centering and smoothing it as necessary. Water-activated stabilizers may also be used with this method. Hoop the stabilizer, and then follow the manufacturer's instructions to moisten it; adhere the fabric to be embroidered.

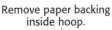

Remove paper backing
inside hoop.

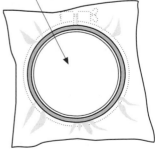

Hooped Stabilizer

Smooth fabric onto adhesive.

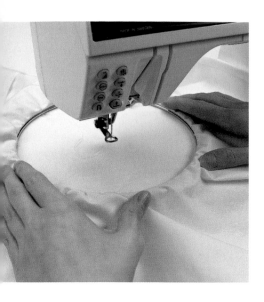

Pay attention to the placement of your hands when embroidering with a hoop.

Embroidering with a Hoop

Embroidering with a hoop is a free-motion technique, so set up your machine by dropping the feed dogs and attaching a darning foot. If you have an extension table for your machine, attach it; the larger area enables the hoop to be moved smoothly, which results in even stitching. If there is a slight ridge between your extension table and the machine bed, try taping 3" x 5" index cards over the ridge so that the hoop doesn't catch on it and jump, causing missed stitches.

Prepare your hoop, using one of the methods discussed in "Hooping Your Fabric." Hold the hoop with your left hand placed at the nine o'clock position and your right hand at the three o'clock position (see photo at left). Do not rest your arms on the sewing machine or table! This makes for a jerky motion and uneven stitches.

Guide the hoop under the needle as you would fabric. The speed at which you move the hoop in combination with the speed at which the needle is moving up and down will determine the stitch length. Run the machine at a comfortable, constant speed and guide the hooped fabric under the needle at a steady speed as well. Moving the hoop too slowly results in small stitches, while moving it too fast results in long stitches. A little practice will render perfection!

FABRICS

I HAVE successfully embroidered on quilting cottons, silks, velvets, woolens, outerwear fleece, towels, linens, sheer curtains, medium-weight drapery fabrics, and denim. Just about any fabric can be embroidered! Fabrics should be pre-washed whenever possible. I do like to use spray starch to add extra stability to lightweight fabrics, such as quilting cottons, silk fabrics, and sheer drapery fabric, before embroidering.

BATTINGS

YOU WILL need batting for the quilted projects in this book. I prefer to use a thin batting and recommend 100% cotton, 80% cotton and 20% polyester blends, or 100% polyester. Each type of batting provides a different character-istic to the finished quilt, and each requires a different quilting treatment and care. Refer to the product packaging for specific information about the batting you choose. Make quilted samples using the batting and the intended backing and top fabrics before layering the finished top so that you can get an idea of the look the batting will produce. Here are some tips about the different batting fabrics:

⟡   Cotton battings require a lot of quilting and shrink when washed. If you prefer quilts with an old-fashioned puckered look, do not preshrink the fabric if you preshrink the batting and vice versa. By not preshrinking, you'll end up with embroidered motifs that stand out in relief after the quilt is washed and dried. Don't use cotton batting with an open embroidery like that used on "Paw Prints Quilt," shown on page 88, because the shrinking process will cause the areas that are not embroidered to pucker and it may also cause the batting to fall apart. If you plan to machine quilt, pin baste the quilt layers together every 4".

✦ Polyester-and-cotton blends shrink very little and can be used with any technique. Pin baste every 2" to 3" if you plan to machine quilt.

✦ Polyester batting shrinks minimally, if at all, and can be used with any technique. Pin baste every 2" if you plan to machine quilt.

Fusible battings are available in cotton, polyester, and a cotton-and-polyester blend. Because they are fuse-basted to the quilt top and backing, and can be repositioned, you'll save lots of time during the basting process. Pay attention to heat settings recommended by the manufacturer.

Allow your batting to relax before assembling the quilt. Take the batting out of the bag and unfold it the day before layering, or place it in the dryer with a damp cloth and let it tumble on the air setting for a while.

STABILIZERS

STABILIZERS, IN combination with a hoop, are the cornerstones on which to build your embroidery. They support the dense stitching of embroidery and prevent the project from puckering and distorting.

The stitch density and the fabric on which you are embroidering will determine the type of stabilizer to use. Stitch density is a term used to describe the number of thread rows and stitches in an embroidery design. A design that is delicate and airy has less stitching and will require less stabilizing. A design that is heavily embroidered requires a heavier stabilizer or multiple layers of a lighter-weight stabilizer. In a design with low stitch density, such as the jabot window dressing on page 54, you'll need only spray starch and hooping. For other projects, such as the jumper on page 65, the fabric is heavy enough to support embroidery with just hooping and no stabilizer. Sometimes you will need to use more than one layer of stabilizer or a combination of stabilizers to achieve the best results.

Stabilizers positioned under the fabric are called backings, and stabilizers placed on top of the fabric are called toppings or toppers. Backings support the embroidery design and help prevent fabric distortion. They can be temporary or permanent. Toppings are used on top of napped fabrics to prevent the threads from peeking through the embroidery stitches. They are usually water soluble and removed when the stitching is finished. The water-soluble variety also can be used as a backing.

The six types of products I use as stabilizers are described in the following list. These stabilizers come in different weights and widths, and some

To avoid heartbreak, always test a stabilizer and fabric together with a sample of the design you plan to embroider.

❖

To lessen puckering, preshrink permanent stabilizers by steam pressing them for 10 seconds.

are fusible. Most are white but a few of the stabilizers are available in black for use with dark fabrics. There are many stabilizers available and new ones are constantly entering the market. Check for the newest products at your sewing-machine dealership or visit sewing-machine manufacturers' Web sites. Machine embroidery magazines offer another good source of information.

✥ **Starch,** which is temporary, comes in a spray type as well as a liquid form that you dilute with equal parts starch and water. I use spray starch for quilting cottons and diluted liquid starch for sheer fabrics, washable silks, and any other difficult-to-handle fabrics. I also use the diluted liquid starch on yardage and large items. To use it, place one cup of starch and one cup of water in a sink or pan. Fold the fabric into a manageable-size square and submerge it in the liquid. Make sure all the fabric is wet, and then hang it up to drip-dry. An expandable tension curtain rod installed above the bathtub is an ideal clothesline for this purpose. When the fabric is dry, press it. Usually, an additional stabilizer is used in combination with hooping.

✥ **Fusible interfacings** are used as backings. They are permanent and great for stabilizing garment fabrics and other lightweight to medium-weight fabrics. Knit, woven, and nonwoven fusible interfacings are available, but make a test sample before embroidering the actual product to make sure the finished result will be pleasing. Interfacings give the fabric body and discourage wrinkling, but using the incorrect one can make the item stiffer than desired. When using a knit interfacing with a stretchy fabric, place the stretch of the interfacing perpendicular to the stretch of the fabric to create stability similar to a woven. Preshrink all interfacings. Follow the manufacturer's instructions for preshrinking and applying interfacing to the fabric.

✥ **Cut-away stabilizers** are permanent and good to use as backings when embroidering knit fabrics and woven fabrics that stretch. They come in different weights, and some are available in black. After the design is embroidered, the excess stabilizer around the design is cut away. Trim the stabilizer no closer than ¼" to prevent stitches from pulling out. Heavyweight cutaway stabilizer is an easy-to-use, all-purpose stabilizer that will provide good results with densely stitched designs. Light and medium weights can be used in multiple layers to get the same result. There are also cut-away stabilizers available that control show-through in lightweight fabrics and are particularly soft next to the skin.

✥ **Tear-away stabilizers** are permanent and used as backings on woven fabrics that have no stretch. They come in light and medium weights and are available in black and white. Use lightweight tear-away stabilizer for delicate, lightweight fabrics; use the medium weight for just about anything else. Use multiple layers for best results. There are also iron-on tear-away stabilizers, a water-activated fusible tear-away, and an adhesive-backed

TIP

✥

When using multiple stabilizer layers, gently remove one layer at a time rather than trying to remove all layers at once.

tear-away available for those who wish to avoid temporary spray adhesives. The adhesive-backed tear-away stabilizer is good for fabrics that are too small to be hooped, such as collars, or fabrics such as velvet that can be damaged by hooping and require an alternative method (refer to "The Hoopless Method" on page 15). Gently remove excess stabilizer to prevent pulling stitches from the design.

 Water-soluble stabilizers are temporary and dissolve in water. They serve mainly as a topper, but they can be used as a backing also. Store these products in a sealed plastic bag to keep them from dissolving in humidity. As of this writing, water-soluble stabilizers come in four forms: clear plastic-type films both with and without adhesive, an opaque nonwoven, and a paper.

Film-type water-soluble stabilizer comes in several weights, from thin to super thick. Multiple layers may be used as needed. This type is generally used as a topping for knits as well as fabrics with a nap, like towels and fleece. Some of the heavier films require several rinsings to dissolve completely. Use this product when a permanent stabilizer is unwanted or unnecessary, such as for terry cloth towels. Simply hoop the fabric and stabilizer together or use a spray adhesive to stick the two together before hooping. You can also use the product as an embroidery design guide. Just trace the design onto the film with a pen, pin the film to the item to be embroidered, hoop it, and stitch. This stabilizer can also be used as a base for making lace, appliqués, and thread fabric (threads and fabric scraps are sandwiched between two layers of film, hooped, and stitched together). Use adhesive-backed water-soluble film-type stabilizers as backings for fabrics that are too delicate, stretchy, or thick to be hooped (refer to "The Hoopless Method" on page 15).

Nonwoven water-soluble stabilizer is used mainly as a temporary backing and for making thread lace. It is stronger, takes dense stitching very well, and is not as sensitive to humidity as the films. I also use this stabilizer in combination with adhesive spray for embroidering quilt fabric blocks when I don't want the extra thickness of a permanent stabilizer.

Water-soluble paper stabilizer is relatively new to the market. It can be run through an ink-jet or bubble-jet printer for copying multiple designs or downloading designs off the computer. Use spray adhesive to adhere fabric to the stabilizer before hooping.

To remove a water-soluble stabilizer, tear or cut away excess stabilizer and simply place the embroidered area in warm water until the stabilizer dissolves. Several water changes may be necessary to remove all the film. Water-soluble stabilizers can be used with fabrics that are not washable, too, such as rayon velvet. In this case, let the project sit in the open air for a few days and the stabilizer will crumble. You can then brush off the residue.

TIPS

If the needle creates a hole in the film during embroidering that interferes with stability, just add another piece of water-soluble stabilizer under your work.

With napped fabrics, extra steps are sometimes necessary to keep the fibers from showing through the design. One option is to stitch the design twice. You can also use two threads and a topstitching needle to stitch the design. Or, you can use a permanent vinyl topping product. It comes in many colors to match your embroidery thread. Trace your embroidery design onto it, adhere the product to the fabric, and stitch your design.

✧ **Heat-dissolving stabilizers** are temporary, are used mainly as toppers, and disintegrate when heat is applied to them with a household iron. They come in two types: a woven that reduces to charred flakes when heated, and a clear film that melts into tiny balls. The residue from both types is easily brushed away with an old toothbrush. Heat-dissolving stabilizers are recommended for fabrics that are not washable or that are too delicate for other stabilizers. Do not dampen the stabilizer before use or some of the chemical could be released into the fabric, making it heat dissolving too. If the fabric is washable, wash it after the stabilizer has been heated and disintegrated.

Fabric and Stabilizer Combinations

THESE ARE some general guidelines for the type of stabilizer to use with a specific fabric type. Again, always test your choice before embroidering the item.

Knits. Knit fabrics require a cut-away stabilizer or a fusible tricot interfacing as a backing, and they must be stabilized before hooping. A water-soluble topping is also recommended. The hoopless method (refer to "The Hoopless Method" on page 15) may also be used and is highly recommended for very stretchy knits, high-loft fleeces, and bulky sweater knits.

Wovens. Sheer wovens work well with just being starched and hooped. Loosely woven, washable fabrics need to be starched first, and then hooped with one or two layers of a lightweight tear-away stabilizer that you've adhered to the fabric with a spray adhesive. Or, use an adhesive tear-away stabilizer. Tightly woven fabrics work best when hooped with a tear-away stabilizer that is suitable for the fabric weight. Adhere the stabilizer to the fabric with a spray adhesive or use an adhesive tear-away.

Denim. Denim presents special challenges because it is a woven that stretches. Hoop it with a medium to heavy cut-away stabilizer backing that you've adhered with spray adhesive. If the denim is too thick to hoop, use the hoopless method.

Napped. We've established that napped fabrics do not hoop well, so the hoopless method is in order. Use a tear-away stabilizer for a backing in conjunction with a water-soluble topping.

TEMPORARY SPRAY ADHESIVES

THESE PRODUCTS are a boon to embroidery because they help prevent fabric slippage and distortion between the fabric and the stabilizer while embroidering in the hoop. I usually place the stabilizer, either hooped or not, depending on the method used (refer to "Hoops" on page 13), into a "spray station" such as a lined trash can or a clean, oversize pizza box and then spray it with adhesive. This prevents any excess spray from getting onto the carpet or sewing table. I also use the spray to adhere multiple layers of stabilizer together and then adhere them to the fabric. Carefully follow the manufacturer's instructions for use. Some spray adhesives are highly flammable and need adequate ventilation. Many of them are temporary and may dissipate in 48 hours. There is also a permanent, repositionable spray adhesive available.

SCISSORS

I USE three types of scissors for my embroidery work: an 8" pair of dressmaker shears for all-purpose cutting, a 4" pair of embroidery scissors for cutting and trimming in smaller areas, and a pair of curved-tip spring-action shears for clipping threads close to the fabric.

DESIGNS

SOURCES FOR embroidery designs are everywhere you look: newspapers, magazines, coloring books, clip-art books, greeting cards, and the Internet to name a few. I used the fonts on my computer for all the writing you see in this book's projects and samples. But be aware of copyright laws before adapting a design for anything other than your own personal use.

DESIGN TRANSFER TOOLS

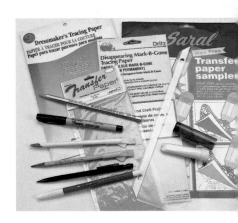

ONCE YOU'VE selected your design, you can choose from several tools and techniques to transfer it to your fabric. Depending on the fabric and the design, one of the following methods invariably works for me. Always test your marking tools on the fabric before marking the design to be sure the marks will come out, and follow the manufacturer's instructions for use and removal.

Light Box Method

If you don't have a light box, any light source, such as a window, will also suffice. This method works well with lightweight to medium-weight fabrics and smaller projects.

1. Trace your design onto paper, if necessary, marking the lines dark enough that you will be able to see them through the fabric.

Tape fabric
over design.

Fig. 8

2. Place the design on a light box or other light source, taping it in place if you wish to keep it from shifting (fig. 8). Lay the fabric, right side up, over the design and tape it in place.

3. Using a marking tool suitable for the fabric, trace the design onto the fabric. In general, a water-soluble marker works well on light-color fabrics that can be washed; a chalk pencil works well for dark fabrics.

Transfer-Paper Method

This method is ideal for all fabrics, especially for heavy, tightly woven fabrics. It also works well for larger projects that are cumbersome to use with a light box. I prefer to use a chalk transfer paper because the marks are easy to remove.

Cut at crease.

Remove bottom and hole-punched side from plastic page protector.

Fig. 9

1. Cut the hole-punched side and bottom edge off of a three-ring plastic page protector. Cut the sheet in half along the fold to create two plastic sheets (fig. 9).

2. Place one of the sheets over the design and pin it in place along the top edge. Trace the design onto the plastic, using an ultrafine-tip permanent marker (fig. 10). Unpin the plastic sheet from the design.

3. Place the plastic sheet with the design on it over the right side of the fabric to be embroidered; pin it in place across the top of the plastic sheet.

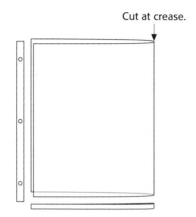

Pin plastic over design
and trace.

Fig. 10

4. Slide a piece of chalk transfer paper, chalk side down, between the plastic sheet and the fabric (fig. 11). Chalk transfer paper comes in many colors; choose a color that will show up on the fabric.

5. Using a pointed object, such as a mechanical pencil with the lead retracted, trace over the design lines, pressing down moderately hard. If you are not sure all the lines have been traced, simply lift up the plastic and transfer paper and take a peek. Go over any faint lines with a chalk pencil.

Template Method

This method works especially well for transferring large motifs to fabric.

1. Lay a piece of transparent template plastic over the design; trace the design onto the plastic, using a fine-tip marker.

2. Cut the traced shape from the plastic. Place the shape on the right side of the fabric and trace around it with an air- or water-soluble marker.

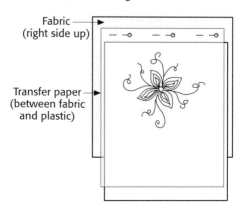

Fabric
(right side up)

Transfer paper
(between fabric
and plastic)

Fig. 11

SURFACE EMBROIDERY *with* THREAD

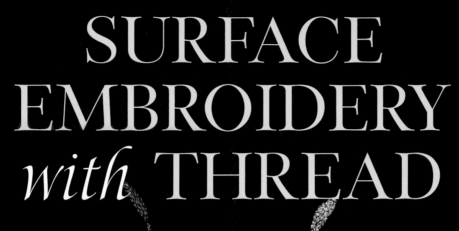

SURFACE EMBROIDERY IS exactly what it sounds like—embroidering on the fabric surface. Use this technique to embellish towels, place mats, napkins, quilts, curtains, wall hangings, clothing, and just about anything else you can think of. In this section we'll cover how to be creative with threads; the next section will explain how to use yarns and ribbons for surface embroidery.

We'll start by learning how a machine's basic built-in stitches—straight and zigzag—can be used to create decorative effects, along with some of the fancier built-in stitches you may have. For zigzag stitches, you'll need a zigzag stitch and a zigzag stitch foot, but in general, even the most basic machine will be able to strut its stuff with nothing special! From there, we'll drop or cover the feed dogs, attach a darning foot, and do some free-motion embroidery. Rather than letting the feed dogs control the stitch direction as when using built-in stitches, you'll be able to move the fabric in any direction to create the design you want.

Any type of thread can be used in the top in any weight that will go through a needle, and even two threads can be used with a topstitching needle. The only trick to working with different threads is to use the appropriate needle (refer to "Needles" on page 11). For the bobbin, use either 50-weight all-purpose thread or bobbin thread, depending on the desired thickness of the finished embroidery. For reversible embroidery, use 50- or 60-weight thread in the top and bobbin.

Select a stabilizer based on the weight and care of the background fabric and the stitch density of the design (refer to "Stabilizers" on page 17). You should also consider how the embroidered item will be finished. Use the following information as a guide, and be sure to make a test sample before embroidering the actual project.

⟡   For a quilt, starch the fabric and use a temporary stabilizer. Quilting the fabric after it is embroidered will provide additional support for the stitching.

⟡   Interface lightweight fabric before stitching. The interfacing will help support the finished embroidery. In addition, a temporary or lightweight permanent stabilizer may be needed during the stitching process.

⟡   For jackets and vests that you will sew from scratch, interface the fabric pieces before embroidering. The interfacing gives body to the finished garment, decreases wrinkling, and supports the embroidery. A temporary or lightweight permanent stabilizer may also be needed during the stitching process. Test several weights of interfacing to ensure the desired drape is achieved.

Stitching Hints

✧ Some bobbin cases have a finger on the top with a tiny hole, or a wire loop. After guiding the bobbin thread through the tension slots, insert the thread through the hole in the finger or through the loop. This tightens the bobbin tension without changing the tension screw and helps prevent the bobbin thread from showing on the embroidery surface.

✧ Lock off stitches by stitching in place five or six times with the stitch length and width set at 0, and then trim tails close to fabric. Or pull the thread tails to the back of your work, tie them in a knot, and trim them to ¼". Threading the tails through a large-eye needle makes pulling them to the back much easier. You can also use your machine's stitch-lock function, if it has one.

✧ Press finished embroidery projects wrong side up on a clean, padded surface. If you need to press from the right side, iron only the fabric around the design and not the design itself.

Built-In Stitch Embroidery

THE BUILT-IN stitches on any machine can be put to use for decorative purposes. Of course, the more stitches you have, the more creative you can be, but you'll see in these projects that stunning results are achievable with just the basics. The stitches used are machine guided, so no hoop is necessary.

Garden Sampler Pillow

Finished Pillow Size: 12" x 12"

You won't believe what a zigzag stitch can do until you stitch this sampler pillow. Add a little straight stitching and a few fancy built-in stitches to create a cheerful garden of flowers.

MATERIALS

- ½ yd. of 42"-wide solid-color drapery-weight fabric for pillow top and backing
- Lightweight tear-away stabilizer
- NEEDLES: 75/11 embroidery; 80/12 topstitching; 2.5/80 twin
- THREADS: leaf green, light pink, medium pink, dark pink, light yellow, medium yellow, dark yellow, dark purple, medium purple, pale periwinkle, bright green, bright coral, light blue, medium blue, and peach 40-weight rayon for embroidery; all-purpose to match pillow fabric for construction; bobbin; 8 colors of pearl cotton that match embroidery threads for braid; invisible for attaching braid
- PRESSER FEET: open-toe appliqué; ¼"
- OTHER MATERIALS: temporary spray adhesive; chalk marker; ruler; three-ring plastic page protector; ultrafine-tip permanent marker; transfer paper; thread-twisting tool, such as The Spinster described on page 109, for making Spinster braid; batting scraps or 12"-square pillow form to stuff pillow

PREPARATION

1. From the drapery fabric, cut the following pieces:
   - 1 square, 12½" x 12½"
   - 2 rectangles, 8" x 12½"

2. From the stabilizer, cut one square, 12½" x 12½". Spray the stabilizer with the adhesive and finger-press it to the wrong side of the 12½" x 12½" pillow-top square.

3. On the right side of the stabilized fabric square, use the chalk marker to draw a line ¼" from each edge to mark the seam allowances. Mark three rows of 4" squares within the seam allowance lines as shown (fig. 12).

4. Referring to "Transfer-Paper Method" on page 22, transfer the patterns on pages 30–31 to the center of the appropriate square.

Block 1	Block 2	Block 3
Block 4	Block 5	Block 6
Block 7	Block 8	Block 9

12½" · ¼" · 4"

Fig. 12

EMBROIDERING

1. Attach the open-toe appliqué foot and insert the embroidery needle into the machine. Set the machine for a triple straight stitch with a normal stitch length of 10 to 12 stitches per inch. Thread the machine with leaf green thread. Stitch the stems on each flower in each block.

2. **Block 1:** Select an oval pattern from your stitch choices for both the petals and the leaves. Be sure that the pattern you select will work with an open-toe appliqué foot; if not, use the foot recommended in your owner's manual. Adjust the stitch width and length to create the petal size you desire, changing throughout as you wish. Beginning at the leaves and

Fig. 13

Start in center.
Stitch out and back.

Fig. 14

Fig. 15

Begin here.

Fig. 16

working to the top of the flower, stitch the leaves with leaf green thread and the petals with light pink, medium pink, and dark pink threads, following the pattern (fig. 13). Lock the stitches at the beginning and end of each motif.

3. **Block 2:** Thread the machine with light yellow thread and set the machine for a medium-length straight stitch. Beginning at the center of each flower head (end of green stem), stitch a straight line that leads to a star-shaped bloom; then stitch back over the stitched line to the center, pivot, and stitch another line. Continue in this manner until all the lines are stitched. To stitch the blooms, position the needle as far left as you can. Set the machine for a wide zigzag stitch and set the stitch length at 0. Position the needle at the center of a star-shaped bloom, and take a stitch to the right over one of the lines and then back to the center. Pivot and take another stitch. Continue in this manner until the entire bloom is stitched (fig. 14). Repeat for the remaining blooms. Lock the stitches at the beginning and end of each motif.

4. **Block 3:** Thread the machine with dark purple thread. Select a decorative stitch for the petals (I used #414 on a Bernina Artista 180) and adjust the length to cover the drawn line, if necessary. Stitch one motif on each guide line, working from the center out. Thread the machine with dark yellow thread. Set up the machine for a narrow-width zigzag stitch; set the stitch length at 0. Set the needle at the far left position. Take 10 to 12 stitches in the flower center to make a small, raised dot, and then move to another position and repeat. Continue in this manner until the center is filled (fig. 15). Lock the stitches at the beginning and end of each motif.

5. **Block 4:** Thread the machine with pale periwinkle thread. Set the stitch length at 0 and the stitch width for a wide zigzag. Set the needle position as far left as possible. Insert the needle at the top of the stem and zigzag in place over the first design line on the right side of the stem about 10 times to make a thick petal. End with the needle in its original position on the stem. Pivot the fabric so that another petal can be created on the other side of the stem. Lock off at the starting point, and then raise the presser foot and slide the fabric to the next petal. Repeat to stitch each petal (fig. 16). Clip the threads between pairs of petals.

6. **Block 5:** Thread the machine with bright green thread on the top and medium yellow thread in the bobbin. Tighten the top tension so that the yellow appears on the surface (fig. 17). Set the needle position as far left as possible. Set up the machine for a narrow-width zigzag stitch with a length of 0. Beginning at the center of the circle, take a stitch wide enough to reach the outside of the circle, adjusting the width as necessary. Once the width has been determined, take about six stitches, then pivot to stitch the next line. Repeat to stitch all of the center lines. For the petals, thread the machine with bright coral thread and bobbin thread in the bobbin. Set the stitch width as wide as possible; keep the length at 0. Beginning at the outer edge of the circle, stitch each guide line about 10 times to form the petal, locking the stitches at the beginning and end of each petal (fig. 18).

7. **Block 6:** This is one stitch you'll definitely want to practice beforehand to ensure that you'll achieve uniform flowers on the pillow. Thread the machine with light blue thread and place the bobbin thread back in the bobbin. Set the machine for a wide zigzag stitch with the length set just above 0. Turn the pillow top so that the stems are facing you. Insert the needle just far enough to the left of the stem that the stitch will be centered on the stem when taken; lock the stitching. Stitch, decreasing the width until the design comes to a point; lock the stitching (fig. 19).

8. **Block 7:** Insert the topstitching needle into the machine. Thread the top with dark pink and peach threads. Set the machine for a wide zigzag stitch with a length of 0. Refer to step 5 to make the petals, making two on each side at each position (fig. 20). Take about eight stitches for each petal and lock the threads before proceeding to the next cluster.

9. **Block 8:** Insert the embroidery needle into the machine. Thread the needle with dark yellow thread. Refer to step 2 to set the machine for the elongated oval shape. Beginning with the larger flower, stitch the center petals. Thread the needle with medium yellow thread, and stitch the outer petals and the petals of the smaller flower. Thread the needle with leaf green thread and stitch the leaves on the smaller flower. Lock threads at the beginning and end of each petal.

10. **Block 9:** Refer to step 3 and use medium purple and medium pink thread to stitch the star-shaped blooms on each flower head. Stitch each petal 4 times.

11. Insert the twin needle into the machine and set the machine for a wide zigzag stitch. Set the stitch length just above 0. Engage the twin-needle function to prevent needle breakage. Thread the right needle with dark purple thread and the left needle with medium blue thread. Stitch on the dividing lines, sewing in gentle curves if desired.

Bright green top thread → ← Medium yellow bobbin thread

Close-Up of Center Petal Stitch

Fig. 17

Fig. 18

Fig. 19

Fig. 20

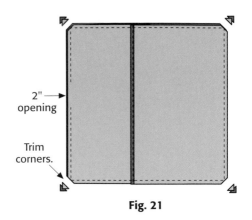

Fig. 21

2" opening

Trim corners.

ASSEMBLING THE PILLOW

1. Using the 8" x 12½" rectangles for the back pieces, refer to "Pillows" on page 109 to assemble the pillow. Leave a 2" opening on one side to insert the ends of the Spinster braid (fig. 21).

2. From each color of pearl cotton, cut two strands, 3½ yards long. Referring to "Spinster Braid" on page 109, use the strands to make the multicolor braid and attach it to the pillow cover outer edges with invisible thread.

3. Insert the batting scraps into the pillow cover until the pillow is the desired firmness, or insert the pillow form.

TIP

❖

Use adhesive-backed Velcro circles to keep the flap closed.

Block 1

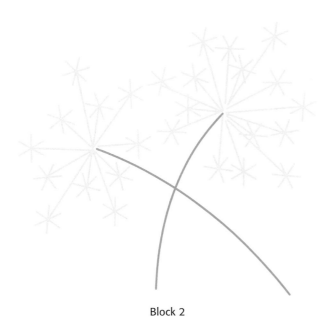

Block 2

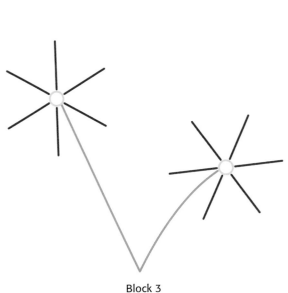

Block 3

Block 4

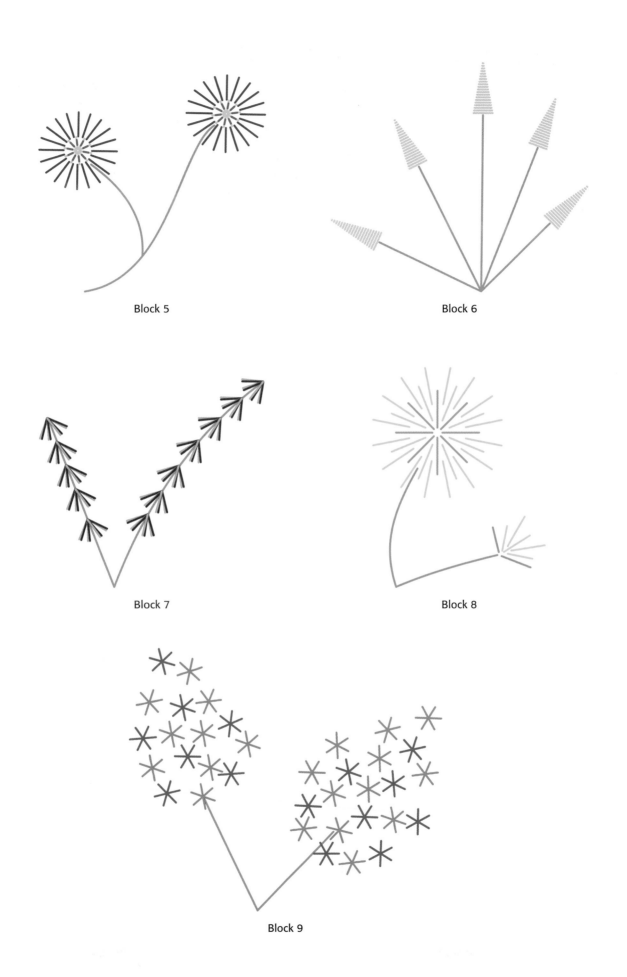

Block 5

Block 6

Block 7

Block 8

Block 9

Free-Motion Embroidery

THIS IS MY favorite form of embroidery because I get to control stitch size, shape, and density. To accomplish free-motion embroidery techniques, you will need a darning foot and the ability to either lower or cover the feed dogs on your machine. Correctly stabilizing and hooping the base fabric is important to success, so be sure you've read "Stabilizers" on page 17 and "Hoops" on page 13.

You begin free-motion embroidery by outlining the design with a free-motion straight stitch. You then can use either a straight stitch or a zigzag stitch to fill the design. The stitch length is determined by how fast or slowly you guide the hooped fabric under the needle. Stitch density is determined by the thread weight and the amount of stitches taken. Heavy stitch density can cause the fabric to pucker if your fabric is not stabilized and hooped properly. This is especially a problem when using closely placed zigzag stitches, or satin stitches, because the zigzag places so much more thread into a design and the back-and-forth motion tries to draw in the fabric. The best solution is to adhere one or more layers of a stabilizer to the fabric before hooping. Make test samples on scrap fabric first!

Free-motion straight-stitch embroidery can be used to create a very airy look, called thread sketching, as in "Jabot Window Dressing" on page 54; or it can create a denser look, sometimes called thread painting, demonstrated in "Purple Posies Pillow" on page 36. You can use straight lines, circles, or any other shape to create a thread-sketched design, but for thread painting, closely spaced rows of straight stitches are used to fill the shape. Straight stitches produce finished motifs that are much thinner than satin stitch embroidery, so there is less chance of the background fabric puckering. To further reduce puckering, use bobbin thread in the bobbin; adjust the tension to prevent the bobbin thread from showing on the work surface. Set the stitch length and width at 0.

The setup for free-motion satin-stitch embroidery is the same as for free-motion straight-stitch embroidery, except you use a zigzag stitch. The stitch length is set at 0, but the width will change depending on the area to be filled. Again, because the stitching is much denser than with straight-stitch free-motion embroidery, the fabric must be properly hooped and stabilized. This technique is a little more difficult because the fabric has to be guided under the needle at a very slow speed to fill the space properly.

Practice Samples

Thread Sketching: Running Straight Stitch Fill

Thread Sketching: Crosshatch Fill

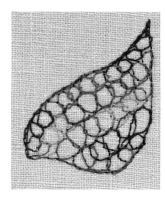

Thread Sketching: Open Circles Fill

Thread Painting

Let's do some practice samples before we delve into the projects. We'll begin by embroidering four leaf shapes with straight-stitch free-motion embroidery. Each leaf will use a different fill design.

1. Stabilize a 10" square of fabric. Transfer four leaf shapes to the right side of the stabilized fabric, using the pattern at right (fig. 22) and the desired transfer method. Be sure the shapes are placed within the hooping area. Hoop the fabric.

2. Attach the darning foot and lower or cover the feed dogs. Set the stitch length and width at 0. Insert a needle that is appropriate for the thread and fabric, and thread the needle. Use bobbin thread in the bobbin.

3. Let's thread-sketch the first leaf with a running straight stitch. Beginning at the leaf base, outline the leaf along the marked line. When you approach the beginning point, stitch into the leaf and make two additional leaves, each one smaller than the previous one as shown (fig. 23). Lock the threads.

4. Now let's thread-sketch with a crosshatch design. Outline another leaf shape with a running straight stitch. Without stopping, stitch horizontal lines (fig. 24) and then vertical lines inside the leaf about ¼" or less apart (fig. 25). Lock the stitches.

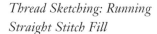

Leaf

Fig. 22

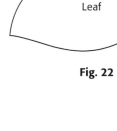

Fig. 23

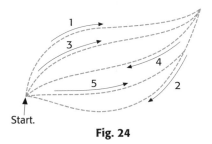

Fig. 24

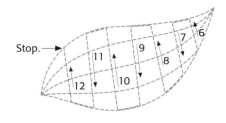

Fig. 25

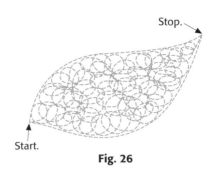

Stop.

Start.

Fig. 26

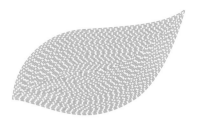

Fig. 27

TIP

❖

"Drag" the thread from one motif to another by raising the presser foot and needle and sliding the hooped fabric from one area to another. This saves time when starting a new motif. Remember to lock the threads with tiny stitches when you start and end stitching!

5. Open circles can also create interesting texture. Outline one of the two remaining leaf shapes with a running straight stitch. As you approach the beginning, stitch into the leaf, creating small circles that fill the shape (fig. 26). Lock the stitches.

6. Outline the last leaf with a running straight stitch. Then continue to lay rows of running stitches next to each other, working around the leaf from the outside to the inside until the shape is completely filled (fig. 27). Depending on the shape and the look desired, I sometimes go around the shape and at other times I sew back and forth in one area and then move to another area and repeat the stitching until I fill the design completely.

That wasn't bad, was it? The more you practice the motions, the easier they will become. Now, let's make some free-motion zigzag stitch samples. We'll use the same leaf motif that we used for the straight-stitch samples, but I'll show you how to fill one with a dense zigzag, otherwise known as a satin stitch, and the other with a more open zigzag design. For the dense zigzag, use either a circular fill or a linear fill.

Dense Zigzag Stitch: Circular Fill

Dense Zigzag Stitch: Linear Fill

Open Zigzag Stitch: Open Rows of Horizontal and Vertical Stitches

A zigzag stitch is created when the needle swings from right to left. Pay careful attention to the instructions so that you begin and end with the correct swing of the needle.

1. Stabilize another 10" square of fabric. Transfer two leaf shapes to the right side of the stabilized fabric, using the pattern on page 33 and the desired transfer method. Be sure the shapes are placed within the hooping area. Hoop the fabric.

2. Attach the darning foot and lower or cover the feed dogs. Set the stitch length and width at 0. Insert a needle that is appropriate for the thread and fabric, and thread the needle. Use bobbin thread in the bobbin.

3. Outline one leaf with a free-motion straight stitch, beginning and ending at the leaf base (fig. 28); lock the stitches. Raise the needle out of the fabric.

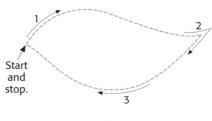

Fig. 28

4. Set the machine for a medium-width zigzag stitch. Position the hoop so that the leaf is horizontal under the needle. Manually rotate the hand wheel so that the needle is in the left swing position; insert the needle into the fabric at the leaf base point (fig. 29). Slowly stitch along the curve so that the left swing always goes into the outline stitch. The stitches should be close enough together that the background fabric is covered. When you reach the point where the right swing of the needle hits the outline, begin stitching so that the right swing always goes into the outline (fig. 30). Continue around the leaf in this manner, ending with the needle in the left swing position at the starting point (fig. 31).

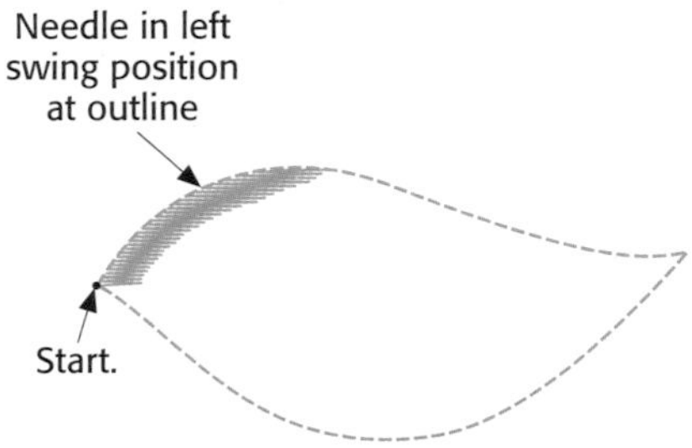

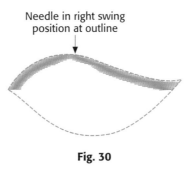

Fig. 29

Fig. 30

Fig. 31

5. At this point you can either continue filling in the design in the same manner, working concentric rows of stitching next to the established row (fig. 32), or you can fill in with linear rows (fig. 33). Try using a wider zigzag stitch to fill the area faster. Lock the stitching when the design is filled.

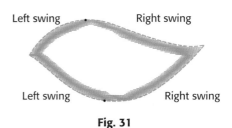

Circular Fill

Fig. 32

6. Let's fill the remaining leaf shape with a more open zigzag pattern. Set up the machine to straight stitch and set the stitch length and width at 0. Outline the leaf with one or two rows of free-motion straight stitching; lock the stitches. Raise the needle out of the fabric.

Linear Fill

Fig. 33

7. Set the machine for a medium-width zigzag stitch. Manually rotate the hand wheel so that the needle is in the left swing position; insert the needle into the outline stitching at the base of the leaf (fig. 34). Stitch across the leaf in vertical rows, moving the fabric faster than before to create the open pattern, and then turn the leaf and stitch in vertical rows again, creating a crosshatch-type design (fig. 35).

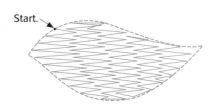

Fig. 34

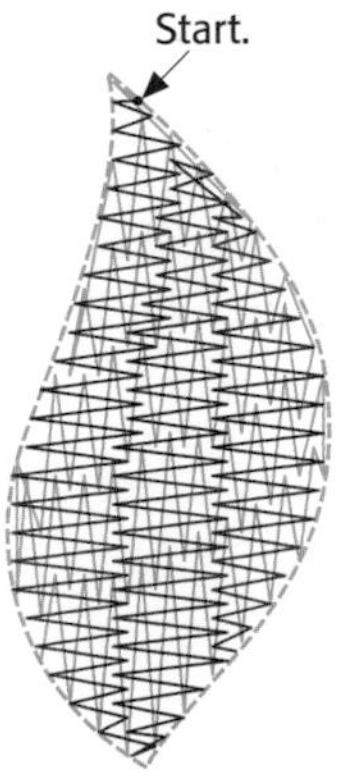

Fig. 35

Purple Posies Pillow

Finished Pillow Size: 12" x 12"

Combine free-motion straight-stitch embroidery with patchwork to make this happy pillow. If purple isn't your passion, substitute it with whatever color tickles your fancy.

MATERIALS

- ⅜ yd. of 42"-wide solid white quilting cotton for pillow top and border
- ⅜ yd. of 42"-wide purple print quilting cotton for pillow back and border
- 12" x 12" square of fusible woven cotton interfacing
- 12" x 12" square of lightweight tear-away stabilizer
- NEEDLES: 75/11 embroidery; 80/12 universal
- THREADS: white all-purpose for piecing; purple all-purpose for pillow construction; purple, yellow, light green, and dark green 40-weight rayon for embroidery; bobbin
- PRESSER FEET: darning; ¼"; zigzag stitch
- OTHER MATERIALS: temporary spray adhesive; spray starch; three-ring plastic page protector; ultrafine-tip permanent marker; transfer paper; chalk pencil; 12" square pillow form

PREPARATION

1. Wash and dry the cotton fabrics. Iron, applying spray starch.

2. From the white fabric, cut the following pieces:
   - 1 square, 12" x 12"
   - 2 strips, 1½" x 42"

3. From the purple fabric, cut the following pieces:
   - 2 strips, 1½" x 42"
   - 2 rectangles, 8" x 12½"

4. Follow the manufacturer's instructions to fuse the interfacing square to the wrong side of the white square.

5. Referring to "Transfer-Paper Method" on page 22, transfer the design on page 40 to the center of the right side of the interfaced square.

6. Spray the stabilizer with adhesive and finger-press it to the interfacing on the wrong side of the white square. Hoop the fabric.

EMBROIDERING

1. Attach the darning foot and insert the embroidery needle. Thread the machine with dark green thread in the top and bobbin thread in the bobbin. Drop or cover the feed dogs, and set the stitch width and length at 0.

2. Free-motion straight stitch the stems and curlicues in one continuous motion, beginning at the bottom of the design and stitching over lines

twice. Fill in the dark green and then the light green sections of the leaves by stitching concentric rows around the inside of each section until the area is filled.

3. Thread the top with purple rayon thread. Embroider the flower petals with the same fill stitch as the leaves, but leave the base of each petal lightly stitched so that the stitches from the center can overlap into the area without creating too much bulk.

4. Thread the top with yellow thread. Beginning at the center of the flower, stitch from the inside of the circle to the lightly stitched area at the base of each petal in a sunburst design until the center circle is completely filled (fig. 36).

5. Remove the embroidered piece from the hoop, press, and trim it to 8½" x 8½", keeping the design centered.

Fig. 36

Assembling the Pillow Cover

1. Attach the ¼" foot and insert the universal needle. Thread the top and bobbin with white all-purpose thread. Sew each white 1½" x 42" strip to a purple 1½" x 42" strip along the long edges, using a ¼" seam allowance. Press the seams toward the purple strips. From the strip sets, cut 40 segments, 1½" wide.

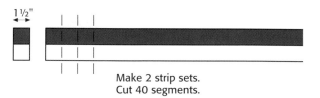

Make 2 strip sets.
Cut 40 segments.

2. Stitch the segments together as shown to make the borders. Make two strips with 8 segments for the side borders and two strips with 12 segments for the top and bottom borders (fig. 37). Press the seams in one direction.

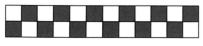

Make 2.

Make 2.

Fig. 37

3. Stitch the side borders and then the top and bottom borders to the embroidered square. Press the seams toward the borders after each addition.

4. To stitch the satin stitch border, raise the feed dogs and set the machine for a medium-width (about ¼" wide), short-length zigzag stitch. Attach the zigzag foot. Thread the top with purple rayon thread and the bobbin with the dark green rayon thread. Tighten the top tension until the green is brought to the surface. Begin stitching ¼" from a corner and ¼" from the seam line, leaving long thread tails. Stitch until you are ¼" from the next corner; stop with the right swing of the needle down, pivot, and begin stitching the next side. Repeat to stitch the remaining corners and sides; leave long thread tails at the end. Pull the thread tails to the back and knot to secure. Gently remove the stabilizer.

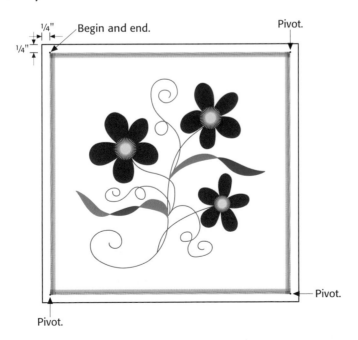

5. Thread the top and bobbin with purple all-purpose thread. Refer to "Pillows" on page 109 to finish the pillow cover; use the purple 8" x 12½" rectangles for the backing pieces.

Fish Hand Towel

Try these quick-to-make towels for your first free-motion zigzag-stitch project. You'll be swimming in compliments in no time at all!

MATERIALS

- Ready-made hand towel
- Water-soluble stabilizers: adhesive-backed for backing, film-type for topping
- 75/11 embroidery needle
- THREADS: 4 colors of 40-weight rayon to complement towel; bobbin or 60-weight cotton to match towel
- Darning foot
- OTHER MATERIALS: screw-type hoop; water-soluble marker

PREPARATION

1. Wash and dry the towel.

2. Trace the design below onto the topping water-soluble stabilizer. Pin the marked stabilizer to the front of the towel, centering the design 1½" above the band.

3. Referring to "The Hoopless Method" on page 15, remove the protective backing from the adhesive-backed water-soluble stabilizer. Place the stabilizer on the bottom of the hoop. Position the design portion of the towel in the center of the prepared hoop. Smooth the towel in place with your fingertips. See second tip on page 19 for additional guidance.

EMBROIDERING

1. Attach the darning foot and insert the embroidery needle. Thread the machine with the desired color in the top, and bobbin or 60-weight thread in the bobbin. Drop or cover the feed dogs. Set up the machine for a medium-width zigzag stitch with the length set at 0.

2. Slowly stitch with the desired color to fill each design area with dense zigzag stitches. Work the large areas of each color first, and then go back and fill in small details.

3. Remove the stabilizers.

Snowflake Floor Pillow

Finished Pillow Size: 26" x 26"

Floor pillows are great when lots of company comes to visit and seating is limited, or when you're just enjoying a relaxing night of watching TV. This pillow features a snowflake, but you can use any design that fits your decor or the season.

MATERIALS

- 2 yds. of 42"-wide dark blue quilting cotton for pillow top and pillow back
- 1 yd. of 42"-wide muslin for pillow-top backing
- Lightweight tear-away stabilizer
- 75/11 embroidery needle
- THREADS: 1 large spool of white 40-weight rayon for embroidery; white and dark blue all-purpose for bobbin and construction; smoke invisible for quilting
- PRESSER FEET: darning; walking
- 30" x 30" square of thin batting
- OTHER MATERIALS: spray starch; 6" x 24" acrylic ruler; 1" x 6" acrylic ruler; chalk wheel with white chalk; template plastic; black ultrafine-tip permanent marker; temporary spray adhesive; white chalk pencil; 7" hoop; 26" pillow form

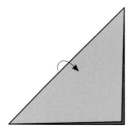

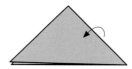

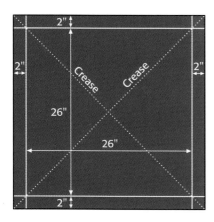

Fig. 38

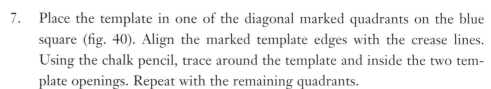

Fig. 39

PREPARATION

1. Wash and dry the quilting cotton and muslin. Iron the fabrics, applying spray starch to the quilting cotton.

2. From the dark blue, cut the following pieces:
   - 1 square, 30" x 30"
   - 2 rectangles, 16½" x 26½"

3. From the muslin, cut one square, 30" x 30".

4. Fold the blue 30" square in half along both diagonals. Finger-press the folds (fig. 38).

5. Using the 6" x 24" ruler and the chalk wheel, mark the crease lines. Draw additional lines 2" in from the pillow edges (fig. 39).

6. Trace the one-quarter snowflake pattern on page 47 onto the template plastic and cut it out.

7. Place the template in one of the diagonal marked quadrants on the blue square (fig. 40). Align the marked template edges with the crease lines. Using the chalk pencil, trace around the template and inside the two template openings. Repeat with the remaining quadrants.

Fig. 40

8. With spray adhesive, apply stabilizer to the wrong side of the marked pillow-top square. Overlap pieces ½" as necessary to cover the embroidery area (fig. 41).

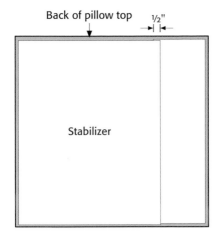

Fig. 41

EMBROIDERING

1. Attach the darning foot and insert the embroidery needle. Thread the machine with the white rayon on top and white all-purpose thread in the bobbin. Set the stitch length and width at 0. Hoop one quadrant of the design.

2. For each quadrant of the design, outline the outer edges and opening edges with free-motion straight stitching.

3. Set the machine for a medium-width zigzag stitch; leave the length set at 0. Moving quickly, stitch the inside of the snowflake with an open free-motion zigzag stitch, going over each area twice in opposite directions; lock the stitching.

4. Remove the fabric from the hoop. Gently remove the stabilizer and lightly press the fabric from the wrong side.

QUILTING

1. Randomly draw small star designs on the pillow top like the ones shown below, using the 1" x 6" ruler and the chalk wheel. Keep the stars at least 1" from the marked seam line.

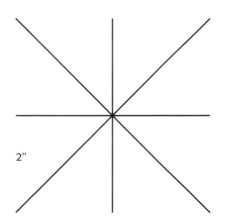
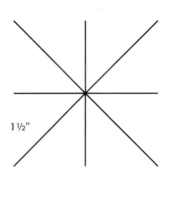
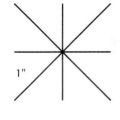

2. Referring to "Assembling the Layers" on page 104, use the adhesive spray to layer the pillow top with batting and the muslin square.

3. Set the stitch width and length at 0. Thread the top with smoke invisible thread.

NOTE

The quilting part of this project can be skipped if the pillow-top fabric is interfaced with a woven fusible interfacing prior to embroidery. This fabric needs support for the embroidery, and interfacing in combination with a stabilizer will work, or you can stabilize the piece with batting and quilting later.

4. Referring to "Quilting" on page 105, stipple stitch in the snowflake openings. After all the openings are stitched, use a meandering stitch to quilt the remainder of the background. It's OK to stitch over the small snowflake markings.

5. Thread the machine with the white rayon on top and the white all-purpose thread in the bobbin. Embroider the small stars. Beginning in the center of each motif, stitch out to the end of a line and then back to the center. Repeat until all eight lines are double stitched; stop with the needle down at the center of the motif. Now stitch shorter lines between the longer lines, using the same back-and-forth technique. Lock stitches.

ASSEMBLING THE PILLOW COVER

1. Serge or zigzag stitch the pillow-top raw edges. Wash and dry the pillow top, and then trim the piece to 26½" x 26½", keeping the design centered.

2. Refer to "Pillows" on page 109 to complete the pillow, using the walking foot and the blue thread to stitch the blue 16½" x 26½" back pieces to the front.

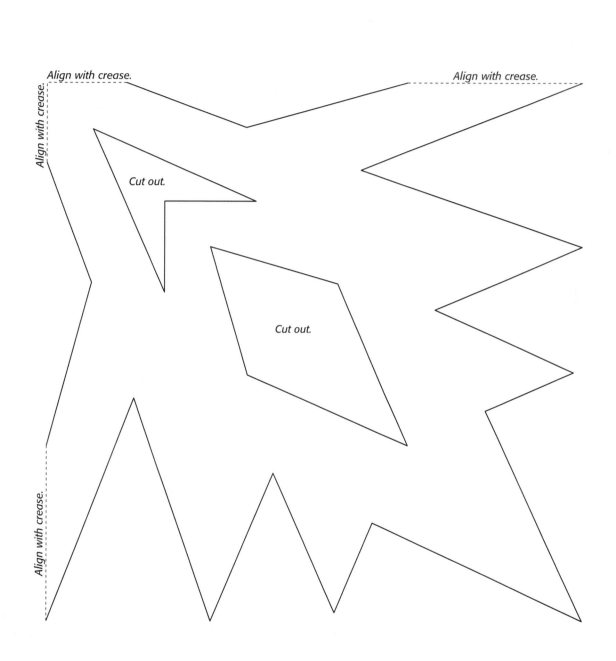

Align with crease.

Align with crease.

Align with crease.

Cut out.

Cut out.

Align with crease.

Hearts and Flowers Wall Hanging

Finished Wall Hanging Size: 33½" x 33½"

*Combine straight-stitch and zigzag-stitch free-motion embroidery with fusible appliqué and a few built-in stitches
to make this easy wall hanging. It's a great way to welcome the warmth and happiness of spring.*

MATERIALS

- 2 yds. of 42"-wide black solid quilting cotton for sashing, borders, backing, and binding
- ⅜ yd. *each* of 42"-wide quilting cotton in 5 bright cool-color prints and 4 bright warm-color prints for block backgrounds
- ¼ yd. *each* of 42"-wide quilting cotton in 5 bright warm-color solids and 4 bright cool-color solids for appliqués
- Lightweight tear-away stabilizer
- NEEDLES: 75/11 embroidery; 75/11 quilting
- THREADS: assorted colors of 40-weight rayon to match block background fabrics for embroidery; bobbin; black all-purpose for construction; invisible for quilting
- 1 yd. of lightweight paper-backed fusible web
- PRESSER FEET: darning; open-toe appliqué; ¼"; walking
- 36" x 36" square of batting
- OTHER MATERIALS: spray starch; 5" hoop; three-ring plastic sheet protector; ultrafine-tip permanent marker; transfer paper; chalk pencil; mechanical pencil; temporary spray adhesive

PREPARATION

1. Wash and dry all fabrics. Iron, applying spray starch.

2. From *each* of the block background fabrics, cut one square, 9½" x 9½".

3. From the black fabric, cut the following pieces:
   - 8 strips, 2" x 42"; crosscut the strips to make:
     - 6 strips, 2" x 9½"
     - 4 strips, 2" x 30½"
     - 2 strips, 2" x 33½"
   - 1 square, 36" x 36"
   - 4 strips, 2½" x 42"

APPLIQUÉING

1. Using the pattern on page 52, trace nine hearts onto the paper side of the fusible web, leaving a small amount of space between each shape. Cut out each heart, leaving a ¼" margin (fig. 42).

2. Following the manufacturer's instructions, fuse one heart to the wrong side of each appliqué fabric. Cut out the hearts on the drawn line.

3. Center each warm-color heart on a cool-color background square and each cool-color heart on a warm-color background square; fuse in place, following the manufacturer's instructions.

TIP

❖

For easier removal of the paper backing, peel one edge of the paper a little past the cutting line before you cut out the shape.

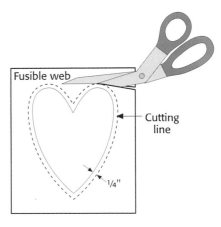

Fusible web — Cutting line — ¼"

Fig. 42

Photo Gallery

JABOT WINDOW DRESSING. *This beautiful and stylish jabot features flowers "painted" with free-motion straight-stitch embroidery and variegated thread. Ready-made, this jabot would fetch triple the price of the unembellished window dressing.*

FANCIFUL PILLOWCASES. *There's no need to settle for plain-Jane cases when built-in stitches and variegated thread can turn them into charming accessories for your bed.*

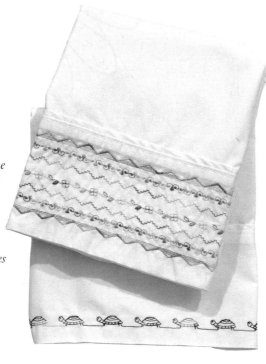

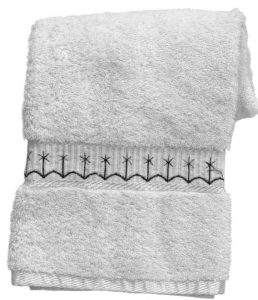

SPRINGTIME. *Built-in stitches create the ground for free-motion stems and flowers on the band of a ready-made hand towel.*

CHRISTMAS QUILT, *31" x 31".*
This festive wall hanging or table covering combines straight-stitch and zigzag-stitch free-motion embroidery to create the holiday motifs. See "Resources" on page 111 for pattern information.

COPY CAT NAPKIN.
The motif from this plate inspired the matching napkin.

FLORAL FANTASY. *Velvet served as the canvas for this jacket with embroidered garden flowers. It is owned by Coats & Clark, Inc.*

FANCIFUL FLOWERS. *Bordered by built-in stitches, free-motion embroidered flowers come to life on a drapery-weight moiré vest. See "Resources" on page 111 for pattern information.*

POTPOURRI BAG. *A variety of free-motion techniques and beautiful threads glisten on the surface of a velvet fabric.*

DAISY. *Thread-sketched circles give an airy feeling to the petals on the flower of this cheerful pillow, while thread-painting techniques fill the leaves.*

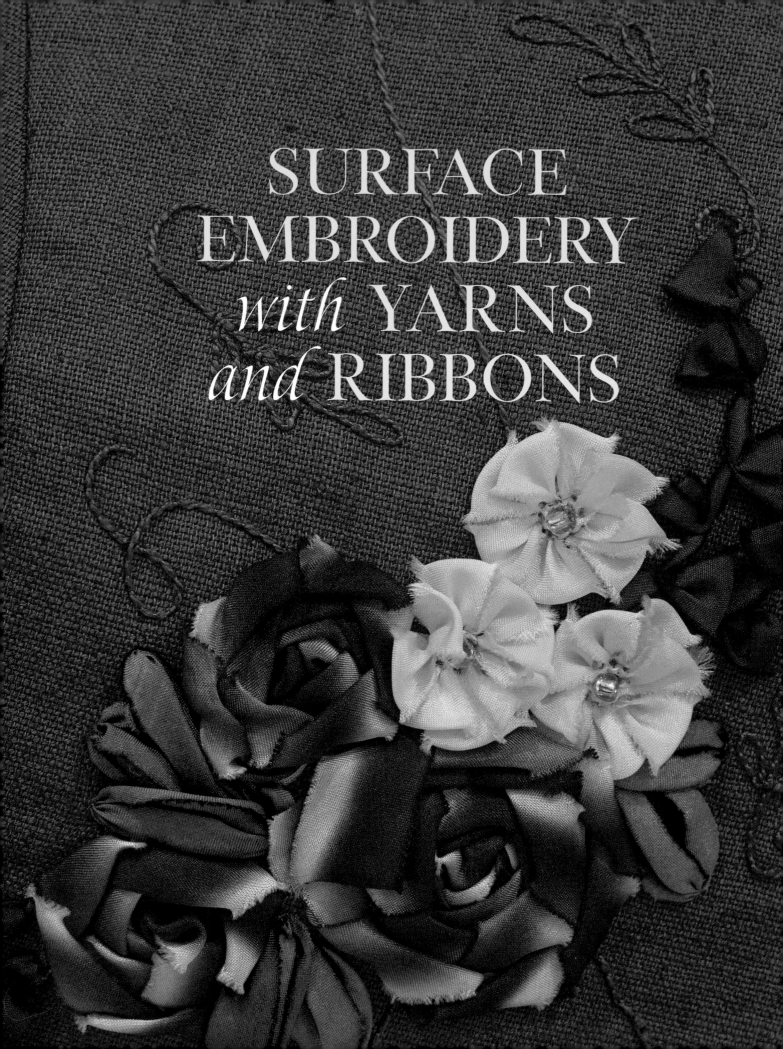

SURFACE
EMBROIDERY
with YARNS
and RIBBONS

I N "SURFACE EMBROIDERY with Thread," you learned to use all kinds of threads in the needle to create embroidered designs on the surface of fabric. In this section, the "threads"—yarn and ribbon—will once again be attached to the surface of the fabric, but because they are too thick to go through a needle, they will require some different application techniques.

My initial encounter with using yarn to create surface embroidery occurred when I purchased my first top-of-the-line sewing machine in 1977. At that time the dealer was offering a class on using a sewing machine to do crewel embroidery. I took the class and learned to use yarn in my machine to embroider stitches that I once had only been able to do by hand. Since then, the technique has evolved to include silk ribbon to create beautiful three-dimensional motifs.

The machine techniques for crewel embroidery and silk ribbon embroidery are basically the same; only the embroidery materials themselves are different. Crewel embroidery works best with soft yarns and braids. Machine-stitched silk ribbon embroidery works beautifully with the standard 4 mm- and 7 mm-wide

FLORAL BELL PULL, *7" x 24½".*
This bell pull is a sampler of the stitches described in this section and was made for Artemis, Inc., to showcase their wide ribbons. The background fabric is broom-sticked velvet. This sampler is owned by Artemis, Inc.

BRIAR ROSE. *This vest is part of a three-piece ensemble I made for a competition. The jacket and vest were bobbin embroidered with small leaf motifs for texture, and then the wide silk ribbon flowers were added (see the jacket on page 86).*

CREAM VEST. *Narrow silk ribbon embellishes the collar of a simple silk vest.*

DADDY'S VEST NO MORE. *This once-masculine vest takes a feminine turn with lazy daisy flowers made from wool yarn and rayon cable. The green thread-sketched tendrils add the finishing touch.*

BERIBBONED HAND TOWEL.
This towel is an easy way to get started with ribbon and crewel embroidery. The stems are created with a simple satin stitch and the flowers are lazy daisy stitches and loops.

FLORAL DELIGHT PICTURE.
A combination of yarns, pearl cottons, fancy braids, and silk ribbons create a great springtime picture. The finished piece measured 11" x 14" before framing.

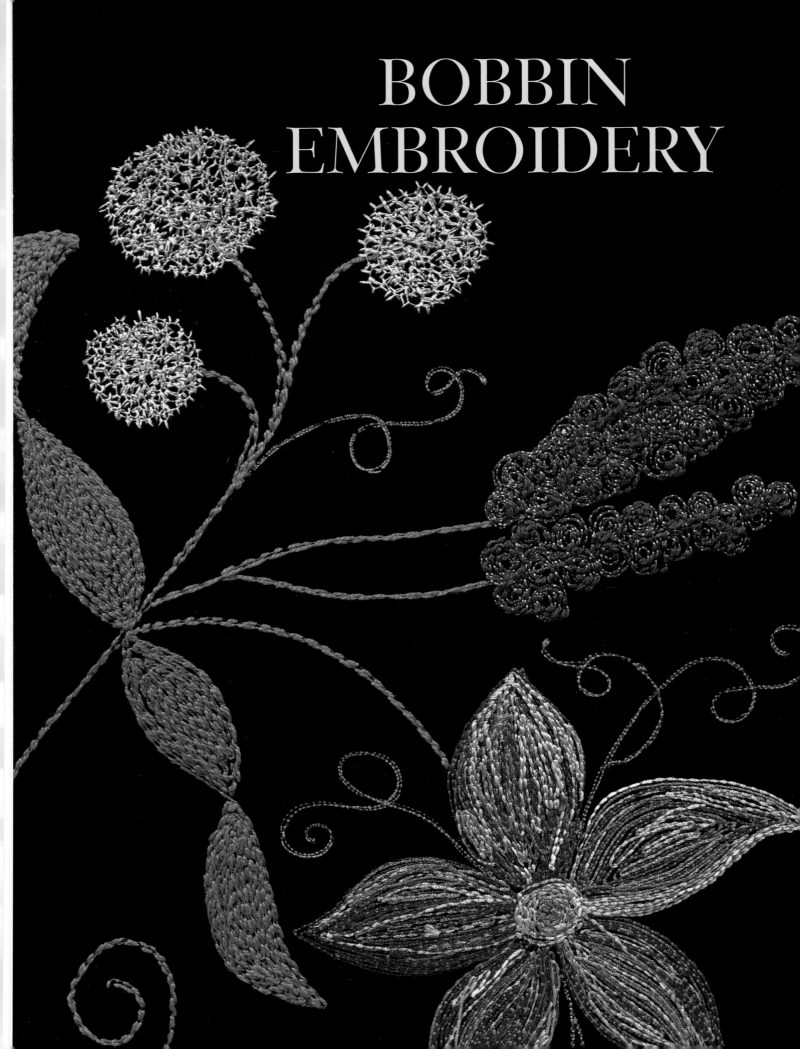

BOBBIN
EMBROIDERY

Tree in a Blue Sky Picture

Finished Quilt Size: 13" x 14½"

With a little practice this project can be completed in an afternoon. The tree is embroidered with the feather stitch and whip stitch, layered with batting and backing, and then quilted and framed.

BRIAR ROSE. *This jacket is part of an ensemble I made for a competition. I embroidered the rose linen jacket with a cable stitch, and I added a silk ribbon corsage to accent the same ribbon used on the vest on page 68.*

BOBBIN PLAY. *This blue silk outfit showcases all the techniques described in this section, as well as free-motion embroidery.*

FLOWERS ON VELVET. *Black velvet brings the bright flowers to life on this 14" pillow. All the techniques from this section were used in some way to create this spectacular sampler. I used cable stitches to create the stems and the orange flower. The pink flowers were made with feather stitches and the purple flowers were made with mossing stitches.*

IRONWORK ON GREEN. *Ironwork decorations were the inspiration for this 8" square pillow, which features a sampling of bobbin embroidery techniques, including the cable, whip, feather, and mossing stitches.*

PRETTY PATCHWORK. *The cable stitch creates the tendrils on this patchwork dress-and-jacket ensemble, while the mossing stitch covers the raw edges of the reverse-appliquéd flowers.*

PAW PRINTS QUILT, *38½" x 49½". Do you know which paw print belongs to which animal? This quizzical quilt of animal front and hind paw prints will intrigue your kids or your favorite hunter. Stitch the paw prints with a free-motion cable stitch, and then quilt the answer in the background of each print or identify the prints on the quilt label. See "Resources" on page 111 for pattern information.*

SPECIAL EFFECTS

YOU'VE ALREADY LEARNED a lot about what your machine can do, but there's even more! This section explores other special effects that you can create with your machine to take your decorative stitching to even higher levels. Some of these techniques require special presser feet, so check with your sewing machine dealer to see if the presser feet you'll need are available for your machine.

Fringing

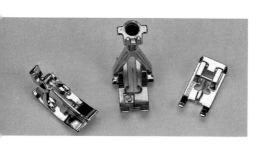

Fringe Feet

*Balanced
Tension*

*Tight Top
Tension*

Fig. 80

A FRINGE FOOT, also known as a tailor's tack foot or marking foot, can be used to create a wonderful fuzzy, dimensional effect. It's ideal for moss, a lion's mane, flowers, and anywhere else you want to create texture. The "fringe" is created by using a zigzag stitch to stitch over the bar in the center of the foot. The resulting loops can be clipped or left in their looped state.

In addition to the fringe foot, you will need an embroidery needle, rayon and/or all-purpose threads, and a tear-away stabilizer. No hoop is required.

Set the machine for a wide zigzag stitch with a very short length. Adjust the tension so that the bobbin thread does not show on the surface. Engage the needle-down function, if available (fig. 80).

To secure the stitching, adhere fusible interfacing to the wrong side of the fabric over the stitching line or stitch over the loops from the right side with a closed-toe darning foot.

Practice Sample

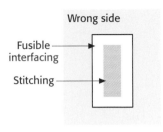

Fig. 81

IN ADDITION TO the supplies mentioned on page 90, you will need one 12" square *each* of muslin and fusible interfacing.

1. Apply the interfacing to the muslin square wrong side, following the manufacturer's instructions. Pin baste a 12" square of tear-away stabilizer to the wrong side of the muslin to prevent puckering.

2. Attach the fringe foot to the machine and insert the embroidery needle. Thread the top with rayon thread and the bobbin with all-purpose thread to match the fabric. Set the machine for a wide zigzag stitch with a very short stitch length.

3. Test the tension by stitching a 2" row. Carefully slide the loops off the foot blade; if you pull too hard all the stitches will come out. If you can see the bobbin thread, loosen the tension until the bobbin thread is no longer visible.

4. Make another line of stitching and gently slide the loops off the foot. Secure the stitches by either ironing a small piece of fusible interfacing over the stitching line on the fabric wrong side (fig. 81) or free-motion stitching over the loops on the fabric right side with a closed-toe darning foot (fig. 82).

Free-Motion Straight Stitch

Free-Motion Meandering Stitch

Fig. 82

DESIGN OPTIONS

Use two different colors of rayon thread through a top-stitching needle for the top. For the bobbin, fill it with rayon thread in one of the needle thread colors or a different color. Tighten the tension until you can see the bobbin thread.

Two Thread Colors through Needle

Two Thread Colors through Needle, plus Tight Top Tension, Gives Three-Color Effect

Mixed Media Pillow

Finished Pillow Size: 14" x 14"

This classy pillow is easy to make in an afternoon and uses the three techniques demonstrated in this chapter: fringing, candlewicking, and gimping.

MATERIALS

- ½ yd. of 42"-wide dark red cotton for pillow top and back
- ½ yd. of 42"-wide bright red for pillow top and back
- 14½" x 14½" square of fusible woven interfacing
- NEEDLES: 80/12 topstitching; 70/10 Sharp
- THREADS: dark red and bright red 40-weight rayon for embroidery; red all-purpose for bobbin; crochet for gimping
- PRESSER FEET: fringing; closed-toe darning; candlewicking or open-toe appliqué; gimping or open-toe appliqué
- OTHER MATERIALS: spray starch; chalk wheel; 14" pillow form

PREPARATION

1. Wash the cotton fabrics. Iron, applying spray starch.

2. From *each* of the red fabrics, cut:
   - 1 square, 14½" x 14½"
   - 1 rectangle, 9½" x 14½"

3. Place the red squares together, right sides up. Using a rotary cutter, cut the squares in half as shown, making a gently curving line (fig. 83).

4. Place the interfacing on a flat surface with the fusible side up. With right sides facing up, lay the top portion of the top cut square and the bottom portion of the bottom cut square on the interfacing, butting the curved edges to form a complete square (fig. 84). Fuse the fabrics to the interfacing, following the manufacturer's instructions.

5. With the chalk wheel, refer to figure 84 to draw the detail lines randomly on the right side of the fused square.

EMBROIDERING

1. Refer to "Practice Sample" on page 91 to set up the machine for the fringing technique. Thread the machine with both red rayon threads on top and all-purpose thread in the bobbin. Set the machine for the widest stitch width and a very short stitch length. Make a test sample to make sure the stitches are very close together but not so close that they pile up on top of each other. When you are satisfied with the results, stitch over the pillow-top butted edges.

2. Attach the closed-toe darning foot and lower the feed dogs. Stitch over the loops with a meandering straight stitch to hold the loops in place.

3. Refer to "Practice Sample" on page 94 to set up the machine for candle-wicking. Using dark red thread on the bright red fabric portion and the bright red thread on the dark red fabric portion, stitch the lines indicated for candlewicking in figure 84.

4. Refer to "Practice Sample" on page 99 to set up the machine for gimping. Stitch the lines indicated for gimping in figure 84, using dark red thread on the bright red fabric portion and bright red thread on the dark red fabric portion.

ASSEMBLING THE PILLOW

Refer to "Pillows" on page 109 to assemble the pillow; use the 9½" x 14½" rectangles for the backing pieces.

Fig. 83

Candlewicking — Gimping — Fringing

Fig. 84

TIP

❖

Cut a second 14½" square of interfacing and make a second pillow with the leftover fabric pieces!

Candlewicking

L ET'S TAKE A time-consuming hand-stitching technique and convert it to a timesaving machine-stitching technique. Some companies have a special candlewicking foot, but an open-toe appliqué foot will work just as well.

The basic stitch is composed of two straight stitches followed by seven zigzag stitches stitched in place that form a "dot." You can vary the length and number of the straight stitches and the width and number of the zigzag stitches to create different looks. If possible, once you establish the stitch, program it into your machine to make stitching go faster. Engage the needle-down function, if available.

Candlewick Foot

Any thread that can go through a needle will work for this technique, but an all-purpose thread replicates the original handmade stitch the best. Try other types to see what results you prefer. To stabilize the fabric, use spray starch when you iron the fabric and place a light-weight, removable stabilizer that is suitable for the fabric type and weight on the fabric wrong side before you embroider.

Practice Sample

T HIS WON'T TAKE long, but it will help you establish the stitch pattern. Try several types of thread to see the different results. To make the sample, you will need a square of quilting cotton and a same-size square of nonwoven water-soluble or tear-away stabilizer.

1. Attach the candlewicking or appliqué foot, and insert a Sharp needle into the machine. Thread the top and bobbin with the same thread. Set the machine for a short straight stitch. Make two complete straight stitches.

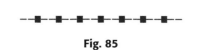

Fig. 85

2. Set the machine for a medium-width zigzag stitch; set the length at 0. Take seven stitches to make the dot (fig. 85).

3. Repeat the straight and zigzag stitch sequence until you achieve the desired line length.

Blue Flowers Table Runner

Finished Table Runner Size: 16½" x 38½"
Combine beautiful old-fashioned candlewicking, free-motion embroidered tendrils, and fringing to complete a classic blue-and-white table runner.

MATERIALS

- 1 yd. of 42"-wide white quilting cotton for blocks and backing
- ⅝ yd. of 42"-wide blue quilting cotton for border and binding
- 19" x 41" rectangle of batting
- 80/12 Sharp needle
- THREADS: blue and white all-purpose for construction; clear and smoke invisible for quilting
- PRESSER FEET: candlewicking or appliqué; fringe; ¼"; walking; darning
- OTHER MATERIALS: spray starch; spray adhesive; nonwoven water-soluble stabilizer; 7" hoop; three-ring plastic page protector; black ultrafine-tip permanent marker; transfer paper; mechanical pencil; toothpick

PREPARATION

1. Wash the cotton fabrics. Iron, applying spray starch.

2. From the white fabric, cut the following pieces:
   - 3 squares, 11½" x 11½"
   - 1 rectangle, 19" x 41"

3. From the blue fabric, cut the following pieces:
   - 2 strips, 3" x 33½"
   - 2 strips, 3" x 16½"
   - 3 strips, 2½" x 42"

4. Referring to "Transfer-Paper Method" on page 22, transfer the floral design on page 98 to the center of each white 11½" square.

5. From the water-soluble stabilizer, cut three squares, 11½" x 11½". Following the manufacturer's instructions, use the spray adhesive to adhere one square to the wrong side of each marked white square.

EMBROIDERING

Fig. 86

1. Refer to "Practice Sample" for candlewicking on page 94 to set up the machine for the candlewicking technique. Thread the top and bobbin with blue thread. For each block, begin at the outside of the center circle and stitch the petal lines, using the candlewicking technique. Place a dot at the turn point of each petal, extending beyond the petal line if necessary (fig. 86).

2. Refer to "Free-Motion Embroidery" on page 32 to set up the machine for free-motion straight stitching. Hoop one of the blocks. Beginning at the outside of the center ring, stitch each leaf detail line and then stitch back to the center over the stitched line (fig. 87). Repeat for each block. Do not stitch the tendrils at this time.

Fig. 87

3. Refer to "Practice Sample" for fringing on page 91 to set up the machine for the fringing technique. Stitch on the center circle outline, using fringing techniques. The fringe foot sometimes presents a problem going in circles because the thread doesn't slide off quickly enough to pivot and stay on a circular line. To prevent this, stitch short groups of stitches and slide the threads off the foot carefully. Then pivot the fabric and start to stitch again (fig. 88). Use a toothpick to hold the previous stitches out of the way. When you have completed the circle, secure the stitches.

4. Gently cut or tear away as much of the stabilizer as possible. Any remaining stabilizer will dissolve when the finished table runner is washed.

Fig. 88

ASSEMBLING THE TABLE RUNNER TOP

1. Attach the ¼" foot. Set up the machine for normal sewing. Thread the top and bobbin with white thread.

2. With right sides together and using a ¼" seam allowance, stitch the embroidered blocks together to make one horizontal row. Press the seams in one direction.

3. Stitch the blue 3" x 16½" border strips to the sides. Press the seams toward the borders. Stitch the blue 3" x 33½" border strips to the top and bottom edges of the table runner top. Press the seams toward the borders (fig. 89).

FINISHING THE TABLE RUNNER

Refer to "Finishing Touches" on pages 104–110.

1. Layer the table runner top with batting and the white 19" x 41" piece of backing; baste, using the desired method.

2. Attach the walking foot. Thread the top and bobbin with clear invisible thread. Set the machine for normal stitching. Stitch in the ditch of the border seam allowance.

Fig. 89

3. Attach the darning foot and lower or cover the feed dogs. Set the stitch width and length at 0. Outline stitch around each petal, and then quilt the block backgrounds with a meandering or stipple stitch. Thread the top with smoke invisible thread and quilt the borders.

4. Thread the top with blue thread. Beginning at the fringed center circle, stitch on each tendril line and then stitch back to the circle.

5. Bind the table runner edges with the blue 2½" x 42" strips.

Free-motion embroidery

●━━●━━●━━● Candlewicking

||||||||||| Fringing

Gimping

THIS IS ANOTHER dimensional stitching technique that will add texture to your quilts, garments, or home-decorating projects. The process for this stitch is very simple. Gimp, or a soft, thick thread such as crochet thread, is placed under the needle and zigzagged over with the thread of your choice. The width of the stitch is adjusted to encase the gimp thread, and the length of the stitch needs to be very short so that no gimp shows through. You can use an open-toe appliqué foot and guide the gimp under the needle by hand. Or you can use a gimping foot, a couching foot, or a braiding foot to guide the thread for you. Engage the needle-down function if it is an available option on your machine.

There are a couple of ways to end this stitch. One way is to design the project so that the gimp detail ends in a seam. Another way is to stop just before the end of the gimp detail, cut the gimp, and then continue stitching to the end of the design; finish by locking the stitches.

DESIGN OPTION

❖

Try this technique with two spools of thread, a double needle, and a multiple-hole foot to stitch two rows at once.

Practice Sample

TO MAKE THE most of this sample, stitch over several types of thread or yarns that you could possibly use for the gimp. Then record the stitch length and width next to each one so that you'll have a handy reference for the future. You'll need a square of interfaced muslin, an embroidery needle, and both rayon and all-purpose thread.

1. Attach the gimping foot or open-toe appliqué foot to the machine and insert the embroidery needle. Thread the top with rayon thread and fill the bobbin with all-purpose thread. Make sure the feed dogs are raised. Set the machine for a zigzag stitch that is just wide enough to cover the gimp thread; set the stitch length just above 0 so that the stitches are close together.

2. Place the muslin under the needle at the fabric edge. If you are using the gimping foot, insert a length of gimp into the clip or hole in the foot (fig. 90). If you are using the open-toe foot, place the gimp under the needle and adjust the zigzag stitch to cover it. Stitch over the gimp. Loosen the tension if the bobbin thread is visible. Hold all thread ends as you begin to stitch.

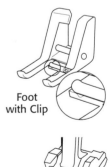
Foot with Clip

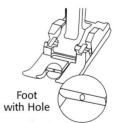
Foot with Hole

Fig. 90

Texture with Lines Pillow

Finished Pillow Size: 14" x 14"

This colorful pillow uses randomly placed raised curves to perk up a plain top. This is a great first-time gimping project.

MATERIALS

- ½ yd. of 42"-wide heavyweight cotton or drapery fabric for pillow top and back
- 16" x 16" square of fusible interfacing
- 75/11 embroidery needle
- THREADS: white crochet; 5 or 6 assorted colors of rayon to contrast with pillow fabric; all-purpose to match pillow fabric for bobbin
- PRESSER FEET: gimping or open-toe appliqué; ¼"
- OTHER MATERIALS: chalk wheel; 14" pillow form

PREPARATION

1. From the pillow fabric, cut the following pieces:
   - 1 square, 16" x 16"
   - 2 rectangles, 9½" x 14½"

2. Following the manufacturer's instructions, fuse the interfacing square to the wrong side of the 16" pillow-top square.

3. With the chalk wheel, randomly draw curving lines across the pillow top.

EMBROIDERING

1. Refer to "Practice Sample" on page 99 to set up the machine for the gimping technique.

2. Cut a piece of crochet thread about 18" long and thread it into the gimp foot.

3. Insert the needle into the edge of the pillow top fabric at the end of one of the marked lines. Stitch over the gimp, following the line across the fabric to the other edge. Clip the threads. Repeat for the remaining lines, using a different color of thread for each one.

ASSEMBLING THE PILLOW

1. Trim the pillow top to 14½" x 14½".

2. Refer to "Pillows" on page 109 to assemble the pillow; use the 9½" x 14½" rectangles for the backing pieces.

Photo Gallery

STARRY NIGHTS WALL HANGING,
*42½" x 15½". This colorful, contemporary
stars and moons wall hanging combines
reverse appliqué with fringing for unusual
dimensional effects and features sun rays
made with thread sketching.*

SHAKESPEARE'S GARDEN, 24½" x 32½".

I designed this quilt for a national challenge several years ago and used Faye Labanaris's window technique to frame the garden scene. I appliquéd all of the background fabrics to a batting base. Then I appliquéd the leaf fabric frame to the quilt top and embellished the garden. Notice where I used different techniques: fringing for the walkway moss, whip stitches for the arbor vines, feather stitches to add detail to the arbor and walkway shrubs, mossing stitches for the cement on top of the stone wall, free-motion thread sketching for the birds and some flower stems, and yarn and ribbon embroidery for all the flowers and leaves. The button birdhouse, frogs, and turtles complete the garden. See "Resources" on page 111 for pattern information.

Finishing Touches

EMBROIDERY MAY BE the fun part of making your projects, but you'll want to finish them so that you can show them off! This section will take you through the steps to finish your quilts and pillows, as well as the techniques for making and applying Spinster braid.

QUILTS

ONCE THE quilt top is finished, it must be layered with batting and backing, basted, quilted, equipped with a hanging sleeve, and bound. Since the quilts presented here are small, follow these instructions for an easy quilting experience.

Assembling the Layers

In this process the layers are assembled and then basted together so that they do not shift during the quilting process. Traditionally, the layers are basted with thread if you will be hand quilting and with safety pins if machine quilting is your choice. However, a temporary spray adhesive can also be used to baste the layers together, which is an especially quick and easy alternative for smaller quilted projects. For an even quicker option, try using fusible batting.

To assemble and baste the layers using either thread or safety pins:

1. Mark the quilt top with the desired quilting design, if necessary. Clip any loose threads on the back of the quilt top so that they don't show through when the quilting is finished.

2. Cut the backing and batting 2" to 4" larger than the quilt top if you have not already done so (the project instructions will include the size to cut). This will give you 1" to 2" extra on each side for the take-up that occurs during quilting.

3. Press the quilt top and backing.

4. Place the backing, wrong side up, on a large, flat surface. Using 1"-wide masking tape, tape the backing to the surface along one long edge of the fabric. Apply tape to the opposite edge, and carefully pull the fabric so that the surface is taut but not stretched; press the tape to the surface with your hands. Repeat the process to tape down the short edges.

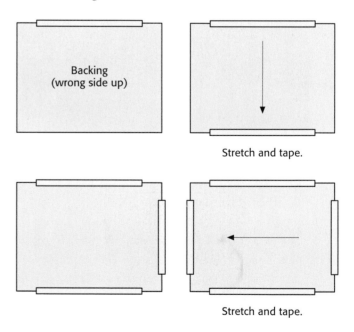

Backing (wrong side up)

Stretch and tape.

Stretch and tape.

5. Smooth the batting on top of the backing. Center the quilt top, right side up, on the batting and smooth out any wrinkles, working from the center to the outside edges.

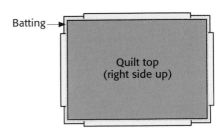

6. For projects you plan to machine quilt, pin-baste with 1"-long rustproof safety pins. Space the pins about 2" to 4" apart, working from the center out and avoiding any marked quilting lines. See "Battings" on page 16.

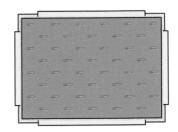

Basting for Machine Quilting

7. For projects you plan to hand quilt, hand baste the layers together. Use a long needle and light-colored thread to take large stitches from the center to the quilt's outer top edge. Baste from the center to the outer bottom edge, and then from the center to the right and left edges. Continue basting from the center out, creating a star-burst pattern.

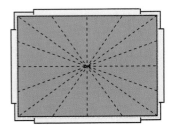

Basting for Hand Quilting

To assemble and baste the layers using temporary spray adhesive:

1. Follow steps 1–3 on page 104 to prepare the layers.

2. Lay the batting on a flat, protected surface. Follow the manufacturer's instructions to apply the temporary spray adhesive to the batting.

3. Place the backing, right side up, over the batting; smooth out any wrinkles with your hands.

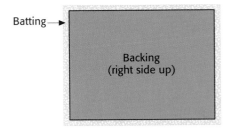

4. Turn the adhered layers over so that the batting is facing up. Apply the temporary spray to the batting. Place the quilt top, right side up, over the batting, and smooth it in place with your hands.

Quilting

This step is just about my favorite part of the process because it means I am almost done. Instructions are given here for two methods of machine quilting: free-motion quilting and machine-guided quilting. Depending on the desired quilting design, you may use one or both techniques to stitch your quilt layers together. If you choose to hand quilt, consult *Loving Stitches* by Jeana Kimball for expert instructions.

Use machine-guided quilting when you are stitching in the ditch (stitching along the seams) or when you are stitching long, straight rows, such as with the crosshatch design. You will need a walking foot to keep the layers from shifting and causing puckers on the back of the quilt.

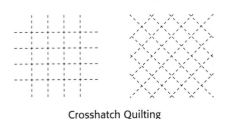

Crosshatch Quilting

Stitching in the Ditch

Free-motion quilting is required for quilting around designs or for filling in a background area with a free-flowing pattern. This technique requires that the feed dogs be lowered and a darning foot attached.

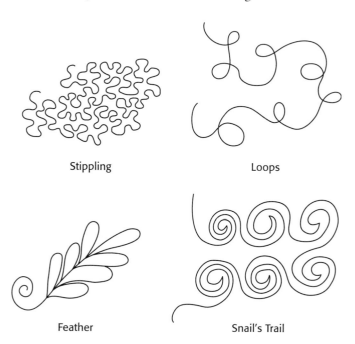

Stippling

Loops

Feather

Snail's Trail

Free-Motion Quilting Designs

For both techniques, use invisible or all-purpose thread in the top and bobbin. It's your choice. Lock stitches when you begin and end by stitching for about ¼" using a very short stitch length. Bring the bobbin thread to the surface and hold on to both threads when you begin stitching.

Machine-Guided Quilting

1. Attach the walking foot and insert a quilting needle. Set the stitch length for normal sewing and make sure the feed dogs are raised. Adjust the machine for a balanced thread tension. Test the tension and stitch length on a folded fabric scrap before beginning.

2. Insert the needle through the quilt layers at the beginning point; bring the bobbin thread to the fabric surface and lock the stitching (¼" of closely spaced stitches). It is best to stitch in the ditch first and then do any other quilting.

Free-Motion Quilting

1. Attach the darning foot and insert the appropriate needle for the top thread. Thread the machine with the desired thread in the top and bobbin. Set the stitch length and width at 0 and lower the feed dogs. Check the thread tension on a quilt sandwich scrap (scrap of layered top, batting, and backing) before starting. Usually the top tension needs to be lowered so that the bobbin thread doesn't show.

2. Insert the needle through the quilt layers at a beginning point (usually the center); bring the bobbin thread to the fabric surface and lock the stitching. Move the fabric and machine at a constant speed to form even stitches. Trace around designs first, and then fill in background spaces.

Adding a Hanging Sleeve

Hanging sleeves or rod pockets are very simple to make, and they are necessary if you wish to hang the quilt. A piece of muslin or leftover fabric from the quilt back will work fine for this task.

1. Determine the depth of the pocket that you need. Usually a 4"-wide finished pocket is adequate for a wall quilt. Double this measurement and add ½" for seam allowances. Next, measure the quilt width and deduct 2" to 4" to determine the pocket length; add ½" for seam allowances. Cut a piece of fabric the determined measurement. For example, if the width of the quilt top is 38", cut the rod pocket fabric 8½" x 36½".

2. Fold the strip in half lengthwise, right sides together. Stitch the raw ends together with a ¼" seam allowance. Turn right side out and press.

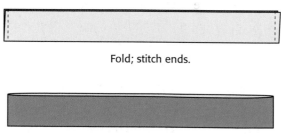

Fold; stitch ends.

Turn right side out.

3. Center the raw edges of the sleeve along the top raw edge of the quilt back. Pin the sleeve in place. Stitch ¼" or less from the sleeve raw edges.

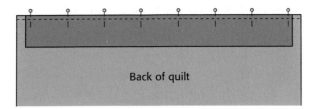

Back of quilt

4. Bind the quilt as instructed in "Binding" below, securing the sleeve in the seam.

5. After the binding is folded to the back and hand-stitched in place, slipstitch the bottom of the sleeve to the quilt backing, being careful not to stitch through to the front of the quilt.

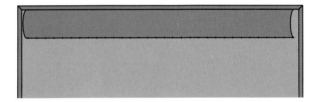

Binding

Binding finishes the raw edges of the quilt. This method produces a double binding because you fold the binding strip in half before stitching it to the edges.

1. Trim the backing and batting even with the quilt top edges.

2. Cut the required number of strips as instructed for your project. Cut the strips across the width of the fabric.

3. To join the strips to make one strip long enough to go around the project, place two strips right sides together so that they are perpendicular to each other as shown. Draw a diagonal line on the top strip that extends from the point where the upper edges meet to the opposite point where the lower edges meet. Stitch along this line. Trim the

seam allowance to ¼". Press the seam allowance open. Add the remaining strips in the same manner.

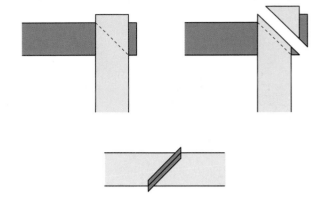

4. When all the strips have been added, cut one end at a 45° angle. This will be the beginning of the strip. Press the binding in half lengthwise, wrong sides together, aligning the raw edges.

5. Attach the walking foot to the machine. Beginning with the angled end, place the binding strip along one edge of the right side of the quilt top, aligning the binding and quilt raw edges. Do not start near a corner. Leaving the first 8" of the binding unstitched, stitch the binding to the quilt, using a ¼" seam allowance. Stop stitching ¼" from the corner. Backstitch and remove the quilt from the machine.

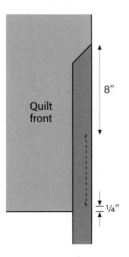

Quilt front

8"

¼"

6. Turn the project so that you are ready to sew the next side. Fold the binding up to create a 45°-angle fold.

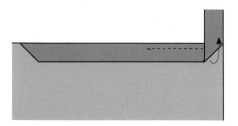

7. Fold the binding back down so that the new fold is even with the top edge of the quilt and the binding raw edge is aligned with the side of the quilt. Beginning at the edge, stitch the binding to the quilt, stopping ¼" from the next corner; backstitch. Repeat the folding and stitching process for each corner.

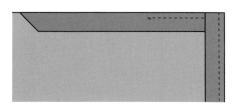

8. Stop stitching 6" to 8" before you reach the point where you began; backstitch. Remove the quilt from the machine. Cut the binding end so that it overlaps the beginning by at least 3". Lay the beginning tail on top of the ending tail. Place a mark on the ending tail where it meets the beginning tail. Place another mark ½" to the right of the first mark.

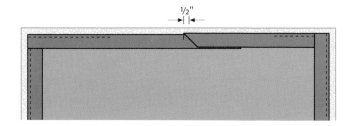

9. Open out the ending tail strip and align the 45° line of a small Bias Square® ruler with the bottom edge of the opened binding strip. Place the ruler point on the mark that was ½" from the

beginning tail mark. Cut the ending tail strip along the edge of the ruler as shown. The ends of both binding strips should now be cut at a 45° angle and overlap ½".

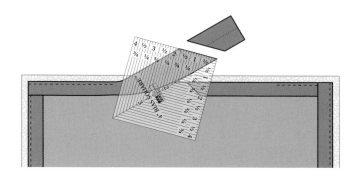

10. Join the binding ends, right sides together, using a ¼" seam allowance. Press the seam open and refold the binding. Finish stitching the binding to the quilt top.

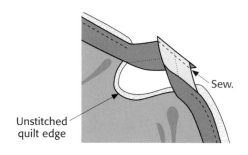

11. Fold the binding over the raw edges to the back of the quilt. Slipstitch the binding to the backing along the fold, mitering the corners.

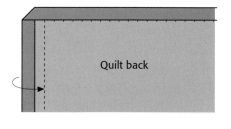

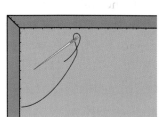

PILLOWS

THIS EASY finishing treatment makes inserting and removing the pillow form a cinch.

1. Turn under one long edge of each pillow back piece ¼"; stitch in place with matching all-purpose thread. Turn under the hemmed edge of one of the pieces 1"; stitch in place. This will be the outer flap of the back cover.

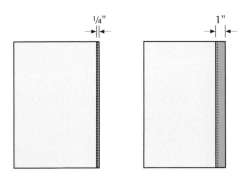

2. With right sides together, place the outer flap over the embroidered pillow top as shown, aligning the raw edges; pin in place. Place the remaining back piece over the pillow top and flap as shown, aligning the raw edges; pin in place.

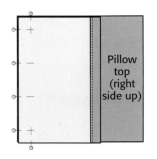 

3. Using the ¼" foot, stitch ¼" from the pillow outer edges, beginning on a side and not the top or bottom. If the pillow will be trimmed with Spinster braid, leave a 2" opening; otherwise stitch around the entire pillow. Trim the corners, turn the pillow cover to the right side through the flap opening, and press.

4. Insert the pillow form.

SPINSTER BRAID

THE SPINSTER is a must-have tool for making your own customized braids. This clever tool looks like the handle end of a fishing rod with a reel attached to the side and a C-hook on the end. Attach the desired threads to the hook, wind the tool, and you have beautiful customized braid in no time at all. Look for this tool at your fabric store, machine dealer, or through mail-order notions catalogs (see "Resources" on page 111).

Select pearl cotton, embroidery floss, yarn, silk ribbon, metallic braid, or any other type of thread or cord. Each type will give you a different look, and combining them will give you even more choices. One rule of thumb when making the braid is that it takes about three yards of a product to make one yard of finished braid.

Making the Braid

To make a braid for edge finishing using The Spinster, follow these steps:

1. Cut three lengths, three yards each, of the desired thread(s). Tie the ends together in an overhand knot.

2. Have a friend hold one end of the thread group, or attach them to a stationary object. (I put a paper clip into a C-clamp that is attached to my worktable, and then I loop an end in the paper clip.) Place the other end into the cup hook on The Spinster tool. Walk away from the attached end until the threads are taut. Wind the tool until the strands are twisted into a cord and the handle is harder to turn.

3. Holding the thread ends attached to The Spinster, unhook the threads from the tool and set the tool aside. Pinch the twisted threads at the halfway point. Bring the two ends together and allow the braids to twist on each other to create a finished braid.

4. Tie the ends together.

Attaching the Braid

To attach Spinster braid or purchased piping or braid to a project, follow these steps:

1. Prepare the project by leaving a 1" to 2" opening in the seam allowance as directed in the project instructions. This opening allows the ends of the braid to be hidden in the seam allowance and secured during the stitching process. Turn the project to the right side.

TIP

To achieve a candy cane effect, cut three strands of thread in one color and three strands in another color. Tie the ends of one color strand together with an overhand knot. Thread one end of the other color through the loop of the first color; then tie the strands of the second color together in an overhand knot. Use The Spinster to make the braid.

---

2. Thread the machine with invisible thread in the top and bobbin. Place an open-toe appliqué foot on the machine. Set the machine for a zigzag stitch with a width wide enough that one swing of the needle just catches the fabric and the other swing lands in the middle of the braid. Set the machine for a short stitch length.

3. Starting at the opening, place the project edge under the center of the appliqué foot. Place the finished end of the braid next to the project edge, leaving 1" loose to tuck in later. Stitch the braid to the project. If you miss a spot, backstitch and go over it again.

4. When you are about 2" from the opening, stop with the needle in the fabric. Calculate the amount of braid needed to reach the opening plus 1" for tucking into the opening. With a hand-sewing needle and thread, tie off the braid at the determined point and cut away the excess braid.

5. Continue to attach the braid. When you reach the opening, tuck the beginning and end of the braid into the opening so that they cross over each other. Stitch across the opening; backstitch to lock the threads.

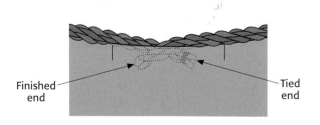

Resources

Check your local craft, fabric, cross-stitch, and knitting shops for thread and fabrics.

Hand-Dyed Silk Ribbons
Artemis Exquisite Embellishments
179 High Street
South Portland, ME 04106
888-233-5187
www.artemisinc.com

Patterns
Pat Nelson
patembroidery@yahoo.com
Patterns are available for the following projects:
"Christmas Quilt" (page 55); "Fanciful Flowers" (page 57); "Trinity Alps" (page 67); "Paw Prints Quilt" (page 88); and "Shakespeare's Garden" (page 103).

Threads
Uncommon Thread, Inc.
Box 338 S. Sharon Amity Road
Charlotte, NC 28211
877-294-5427
www.uncommonthread.com

Web of Thread
19424 63rd Ave. NE
Kenmore, WA 98028
800-955-8185
425-424-2256 (voicemail)
www.webofthread.com

Tools
Clotilde, LLC
PO Box 7500
Big Sandy, TX 75755-7500
800-772-2891
www.clotilde.com

Nancy's Notions
PO Box 683
Beaver Dam, WI 53916-0683
800-833-0690
www.nancysnotions.com

Bibliography

Anderson, Vicki. "Back to Basics: Stabilizer Sense," *Creative Machine Embroidery*, no. 1 (Premiere): pages 10–11.

Country Stitches. *101 Ideas for Machine Embroidery*, Lansing, Mich.: Country Stitches Ltd., 1997.

Curran, Doreen. *The Magic of Free-Machine Embroidery*, Kenthurst, New South Wales: Kangaroo Press, 1992.

Drexler, Joyce. *Embroidery Concepts in Sulky*, Harbor Heights, Fla.: Sulky of America, 1996.

Duncan, Marie and Betty Farrell. *Ribbon Embroidery by Machine*, Iola, Wis.: Krause Publications, 1996.

Holt, Verna. *Yarn Stitchery on the Sewing Machine*, Las Vegas, Nev.: AMI Printing Co., 1973.

McNeill, Moyra. *Machine Embroidery: Lace and See-Through Techniques*, New York: Trafalgar Square, 1985.

Sexton, Jeanie. *Silk Ribbons by Machine*, Paducah, Ky.: American Quilter's Society, 1996.

Sheriff, Martha. *ABC's of Good Embroidery*: Bernina of America, Inc., 1999.

Twigg, Jeanine. *Embroidery Machine Essentials*, Iola, Wis.: Krause Publications, 2001.

About the Author

LIKE MANY OF her fellow sewers and quilters, Pat has been sewing since she was very young. Her first projects were doll clothes made with scraps from her mother's sewing box. She sewed through high school, and then she went on to nursing school, where she became a registered nurse. She didn't start sewing again until she married and bought her first sewing machine. She has moved quite a bit, with each move bringing a new sewing experience.

Pat is a machine-oriented sewer and has been teaching machine-related sewing classes for more than twenty years. She loves the challenge of converting traditional handwork to the machine. In 1977, she became very interested in machine embroidery, appliqué, and other machine techniques. In the past few years, Pat has become quite involved in creating wearable art. She continues to experiment with new machine techniques and enjoys passing them on to her students.

Pat has won numerous ribbons for her wearables, including Best of Show at the AQS Fashion Show, the International Quilt Show in Houston, the Pennsylvania National Quilt Extravaganza, and the Hoffman Challenge. She has also been invited twice to participate in the Fairfield Fashion Show.

Creative Machine Stitching is Pat's second book published by Martingale & Company; the first was *Stylish Sewing*. Her work has also appeared in *The Quilter*, *American Quilter*, *Threads*, *Traditional Quiltworks*, *Sewing Savvy*, and *Creative Machine Embroidery*.